TRANSACTIONS

OF THE

AMERICAN PHILOSOPHICAL SOCIETY

HELD AT PHILADELPHIA
FOR PROMOTING USEFUL KNOWLEDGE

NEW SERIES—VOLUME 64, PART 7
1974

GEARS FROM THE GREEKS

THE ANTIKYTHERA MECHANISM—A CALENDAR COMPUTER
FROM *ca.* 80 B.C.

DEREK DE SOLLA PRICE
Avalon Professor of History of Science, Yale University

THE AMERICAN PHILOSOPHICAL SOCIETY
INDEPENDENCE SQUARE
PHILADELPHIA

November, 1974

Copyright © 1974 by The American Philosophical Society

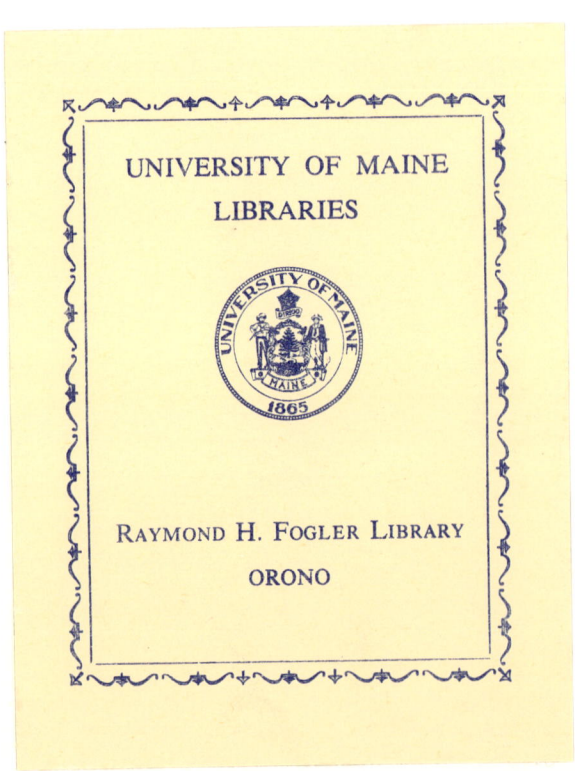

Library of Congress Catalog
Card Number 74-84369
International Standard Book Number 0-87169-647-9
US ISSN 0065-9746

PREFACE AND ACKNOWLEDGMENTS

In a work like this which has been taken up at various intervals and with many collaborators over some twenty years it is almost impossible to acknowledge adequately the help I have received. The record of institutions and fellowships, colleagues and friends, would be virtually coextensive with my biography as a professional historian of science and technology. By its nature the detective story of work on the fragments has been a succession of puzzles and of side-investigations leading into many different areas of competence where I have always found specialists in other fields most generous with their help and patient with a novice.

I have tried to indicate specific debts for help at the place they occur, and in appropriate cases I have asked those who made side investigations to report under their own names. To all of them I am in debt that can only be repaid in small part by the appearance of this study with all the unsolved problems that still remain, the further work that perhaps others will now be able to perfect, and the errors which in the usual fashion are all my own. For fellowships and research grants I thank also those who enabled me to enjoy an I.C.I. Research Fellowship and a Nuffield Foundation Fellowship in Cambridge, a Fellowship at the Institute for Advanced Study in Princeton, a John Simon Guggenheim Fellowship at Yale, and grants from the American Philosophical Society, the National Geographic Society and the National Science Foundation at various times. I am also grateful for an A. Whitney Griswold grant from Yale University for defraying part of the cost of the figures and plates.

My special thanks must go to the authorities at the National Archaeological Museum for many visits where they gave me all the access needed to work with the delicate fragments, to the Greek Atomic Energy Commission and Dr. Ch. Karakalos for the recent radiographic work that led to a solution for most of the gear system.

At the more personal level, like all workers in the history of astronomy, I am indebted to Otto Neugebauer, not only for his own contributions and advice, but also for the clear hard standards of scholarship set by them which give such a special reward for even a most imperfect following. Further debts of gratitude to Gerald Toomer for generous advice on classical matters and interpretation of the fragmentary texts, and to Beverly Pope for her skillful rendering of the line illustrations which are so vital to this monograph. My special thanks also to my colleague over many years, Asger Aaboe, for his patient good taste, and his unparalleled feeling for the history of mathematical astronomy, and to Ann Leskowitz, without whose secretarial assistance I would long ago have been lost.

D. de S. P.

GEARS FROM THE GREEKS

The Antikythera Mechanism—A Calender Computer from ca. 80 B.C.

Derek de Solla Price

CONTENTS

	PAGE
The discovery of the Antikythera shipwreck	5
The discovery of the mechanism fragments	9
Research on the mechanism fragments, 1902–1973	10
The casing, general construction, and dial work	13
The arrangement in depth of the plates and components of the mechanism	20
The door plates and the general orientation and use of the mechanism	21
The accuracy of estimating gear teeth numbers	22
Description of individual gears	27
Description of gear trains	40
The inscriptions	46
The Antikythera mechanism as an historical document	51
The early history of gearing and clockwork	53
The invention of complicated clockwork and the differential gear	60
Appendix	
I. Composition of the metal fragments, with contributions by Earle R. Caley and Cyril S. Smith	63
II. Technical note on radiography of fragments, by Char. Karakalos	66
Index	69

THE DISCOVERY OF THE ANTIKYTHERA SHIPWRECK

By happy and spectacular coincidence the first great discovery in underwater archaeology yielded not only a fine collection of art treasures but also the most enigmatic, most complicated piece of scientific machinery known from antiquity. This singular artifact is now identified as an astronomical or calendrical calculating device involving a very sophisticated arrangement of more than thirty gear-wheels. It transcends all that we had previously known from textual and literary sources and may involve a completely new appraisal of the scientific technology of the Hellenistic period. The unique and crucial status of this object makes it especially important to establish with the utmost certainty all evidence of its provenance and dating. To this end we must first recount the circumstances of the discovery of the ancient shipwreck and of the fragments of mechanism.

Shortly before Easter of 1900 a party of *sphoungarades*, sponge-fishers from the island of Syme near Rhodes in the Dodecanese, left their normal fishing grounds in Tunisian waters off North Africa and began to sail East, towards home. Their party of six divers and twenty-two oarsmen sailing in two *caiques* (cut-ters) seems to have run into the gales and squalls endemic to that area while in the channels between the islands of Kythera and Crete. This channel is incidentally one of the chief shipping routes between the Eastern and the Western Mediterranean. Driven off course they then sought shelter near Port Potamo on the almost uninhabited, rocky and barren islet of Antikythera[1] (also called Cerigotto, Sijiljó and Stus, ancient Αἰγιλία, it is about 1 mile long, ½ mile wide) which lies just midway between the two larger islands, splitting the channel between and creating an infamously dangerous graveyard for shipping, ancient and modern, a place of sandbars, shoals, and sudden currents (see figs. 1, 2).

They dropped anchor about a mile to the east of the port at a place known locally as Pinakakia, a submarine shelf not to be found by name on any chart of the area, which lay some 15 to 25 meters beyond the rocky headland of Point Glyphadia (Vlikada Point, lat. 35°52′30″N., long. 23°18′35″E. on British Admiralty Chart, No. 1685, see inset of Antikythera I, Port Potamo, fig. 3. Compare the map in Svoronos, p. 81, fig. 73). Safe after the storm they decided to explore the shallow rock shelf below them in the hope of finding sponges in the unfamiliar territory. Going to a depth of about 140 feet or 42 meters (35 ells, according to Svoronos), one of the divers, Elias Stadiatis, found to his utter astonishment that a great ship lay wrecked on the bottom. He saw a compact mass some 50 meters in length with all the remnants of its structure and the tumbled amphorae that have since become recognized as typical of these Mediterranean wrecks. The real excitement however was not so much in the ship itself but in a treasure that was plainly visible — a pile of bronze and marble statues and other objects made almost unrecognizable through marine deposits.

Stadiatis returned to the surface with his story and with the material evidence of a piece from one of the bronze statues, a larger-than-life right arm. The captain of the Symiote ships, Demetrios El. Kondos, a former master-diver, then descended to confirm the marvelous find and take rough measurements and bearings so as to locate the site for future reference. The party then returned to Syme without further incident, and spent some six months in the riotous living that was customary on completion of a successful trip and on the weighty deliberation and consultation with elders

---

[1] i.e. The island against (next to) Kythera. It is now officially spelled Andikythera.

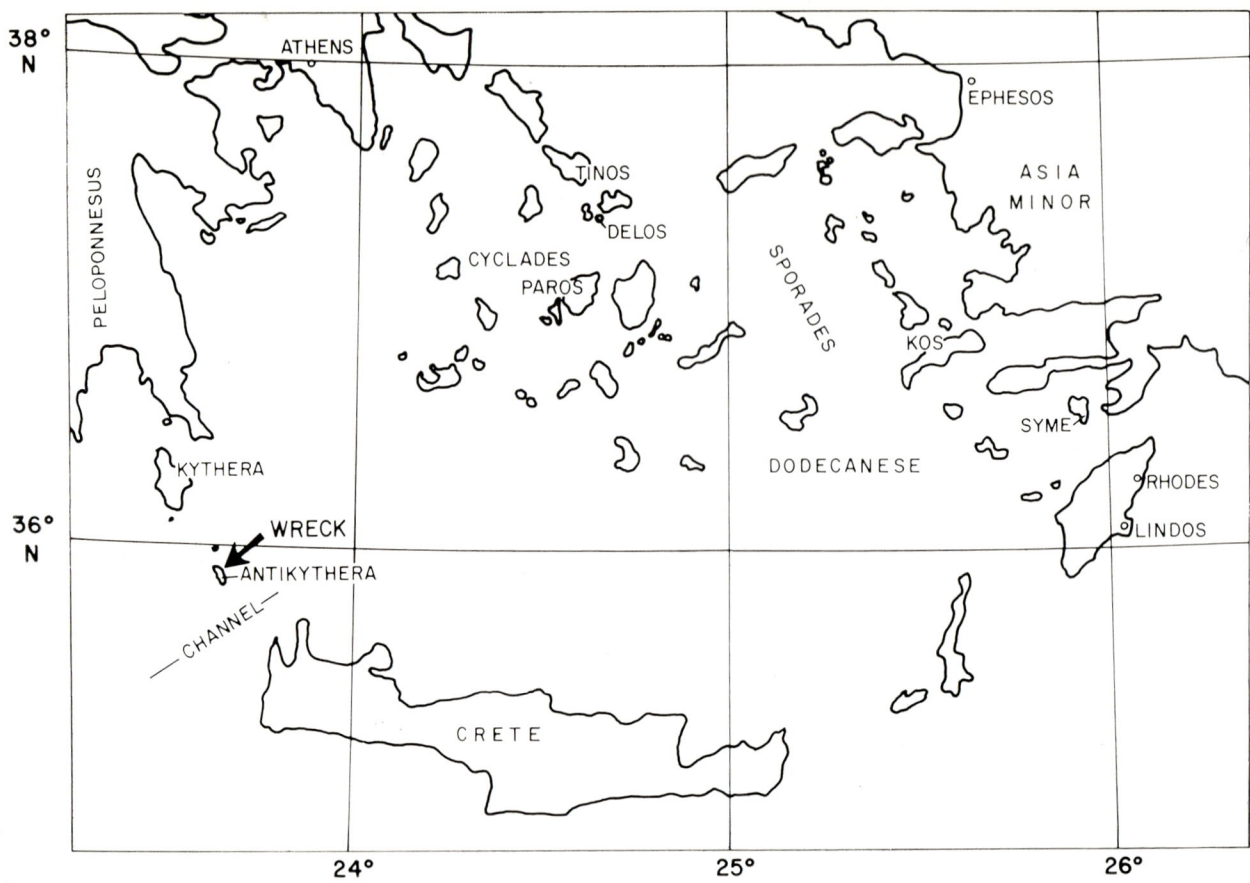

Fig. 1. Map of the Aegean Islands.

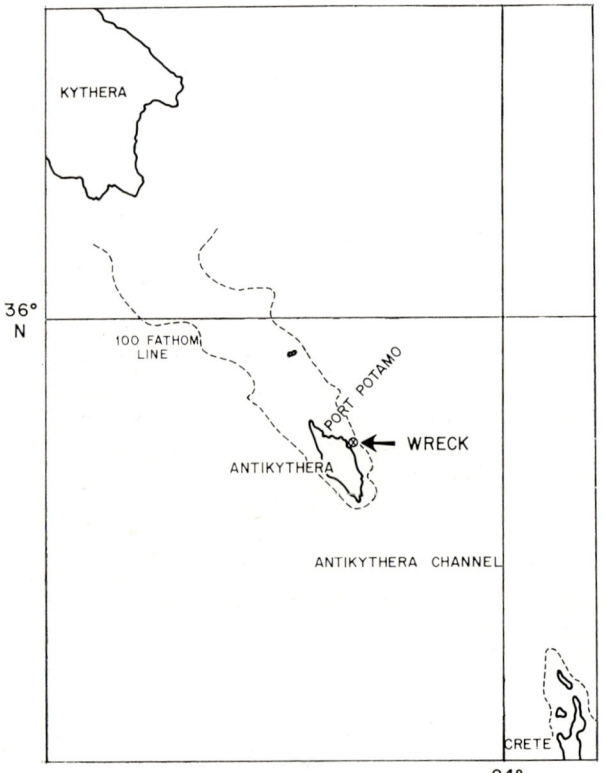

Fig. 2. Map of the Antikythera Channel.

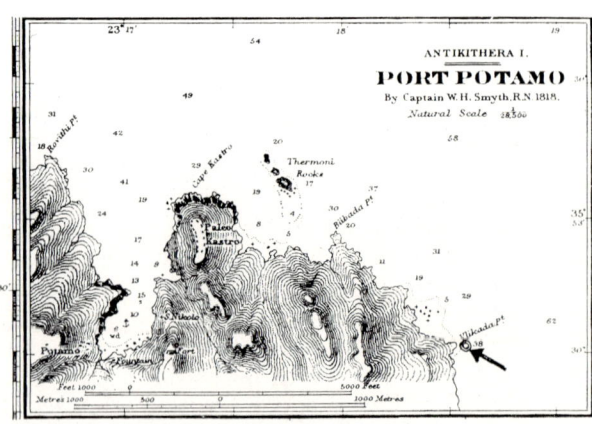

Fig. 3. Map of Antikythera, Port Potamo, showing wreck.

FIG. 4. The sponge-fishers in their *caique* at the discovery site off Antikythera. From Svoronos, 1903.

FIG. 5. Marbles from Antikythera in the Greek National Archaeological Museum store. From Svoronos, 1903.

over what to do about the treasure ship. Deciding to approach the correct authorities, rather than make it an illicit private adventure, Kondos and Stadiatis went to Athens, taking the bronze arm with them. On 6 November, 1900, they were conducted by A. Oikonomu, a native Symiote and professor of archaeology in the University of Athens, to the office of Spyridon Staïs, minister of education and himself a prominent archaeologist.

Action was immediately forthcoming. An agreement was reached whereby the *sphoungerades* were promised proper compensation for the treasures they would recover and hand over to the government, and that a ship of the Greek navy would be at their disposal together with the necessary machinery for hoisting heavy objects. It was also agreed that an official archaeologist would be on board to supervise the operation, and the fishers' friend, Professor Oikonomu, was duly appointed to the special post. Newspaper announcements of the expedition appeared immediately and the fishers' stories were reported.

Because of bad weather it was 24 November before the fishers in their *caiques* and Oikonomu in the transport ship, *Mykale,* arrived at the site, only to find that the *Mykale* was far too large to maneuver so near to the coast in rough sea. It had to return to Piraeus on 27 November and be replaced by a smaller craft. Before this, the fishers made their first trial dive and found the conditions most difficult. Only six divers were available, and because of the water depth they could not go down more than twice a day and even then could not remain on the bottom for more than five minutes, which together with four minutes for ascent and descent entailed about nine minutes of submersion without air-tanks or tubes to help them.

Under these conditions, in a single run lasting three hours the divers had the great fortune to find during that first day a fine bronze head, two marble statues, a hand, a foot, and several smaller fragments. These were borne back in triumph by Ikonomu in the returning *Mykale,* and preliminary statements appeared in the press on 27–28 November. After some delay a smaller ship and another archaeologist were sent out; later four more divers joined the party. All worked tirelessly through foul weather conditions for nine months until 30 September, 1901, when it was felt that the time had come to draw the gruelling expedition to a close. By then, one of the divers had been killed and two permanently disabled by their work, and it had become clear that only with the help of a fully equipped salvage ship could further material progress be made. The one such ship then available in the Mediterranean belonged to an Italian company which would only contract for the job in exchange for half the anticipated finds — a type of compensation that was expressly forbidden by Greek law. The divers were therefore given their reward, a lump sum of 150,000 drachmas (about $5,000) from the state and a further bonus of 500 drachmas per man from the Greek Archaeological Society.

The excavation lasted therefore from the end of November, 1900, to the end of September, 1901, and during this entire period interest and speculation ran high while the recovered objects were brought back to the mainland, deposited in the Greek Archaeological Museum (where they are still happily preserved), and given preliminary publication in the newspaper and periodicals. The principal works of art are now well known, having been given pride of place in that museum for more than half a century. They comprise a superb nude bronze of a young god or hero (the Antikythera Youth) in the style of the fourth century B.C., a fine head of a "philosopher", two fine statuettes, also of bronze and in the style of the fifth century, and the remains of a group of five or six draped male figures. The marbles, leprous and more corroded than the bronzes after 2,000 years under the sea, are also less valuable artistically (see fig. 5); they all appear to be late copies of early originals, made for the export trade early in the first century B.C.

The date and provenance of the important statues have been argued back and forth ever since the first tentative scholarly publication in 1902 and the definitive cataloging in 1908.[2] The shipwreck itself has been assigned dates ranging as widely as from the second century B.C. and up to the middle of the third century A.D. Fortunately the progress of systematic archaeology now enables us to date minor objects with a greater assurance.

As a result of this a new comprehensive study became possible and desirable and this was organized by Gladys Davidson Weinberg and published as a cooperative monograph of the greatest interest and importance.[3] To summarize the chief results it was found that the amphoras date in or close to the decade 80–70 B.C., the Hellenistic pottery to 75–50 B.C. (probably early in the second quarter) and the Roman pottery to the middle of the first century. The agreed limits are thus 80–50 B.C. for the date of the shipwreck, with an early date more likely than a later one. The elm wood from the

---

[2] J. N. Svoronos, *Das Athener Nationalmuseum* (Athens, 1908). N.B. The section of *Textband I* with which we are concerned bears a separate title page: J. N. Svoronos, *Die Funde von Antikythera* (Athens, 1903). Within this is a separate sub-section, *Der Astrolabos von Antikythera,* by Perikles Rediadis.

[3] "The Antikythera Shipwreck Reconsidered," *Trans. Amer. Philos. Soc.* **55**, 3 (Philadelphia, 1965): 48 pp. The monograph contains, in addition to the editor's introduction, sections on the commercial amphoras by Virginia R. Grace, the Hellenistic pottery by G. Roger Edwards, the early Roman pottery by Henry S. Robinson, the glass vessels by Gladys Weinberg, the ship by Peter Throckmorton, and on the carbon-14 dating of the ship's timbers by Elizabeth K. Ralph. I owe all concerned something of an apology for not being ready with the evidence of the present monograph in time to assist their work, and I am grateful for their labours which have now aided my own.

ship itself, dated in the Radiocarbon Laboratory at the University Museum, Philadelphia, using a 5,730-year half life seems to date from 220 ± 43 B.C. and is therefore an indication that the tree was cut more than a century before the estimated date of the wreck.

A recent definitive work on the bronze and marble sculpture [4] considers that the marbles date from the first decade of the first century B.C. and suggests they might well have originated from the island of Delos. Paros and the nearby coast of Asia Minor had also previously been proposed as sources, and it is pointed out there was much war booty at the period of the Mithraditic wars which could have supplied some of the art objects. For the amphorae there is a possibility of Kos or Rhodes. The single lamp from the wreck is of a type found in Ephesos and nearby Asia Minor. The pottery cannot at present be localized more closely than East Greece with a preference for the central part; significantly, none of the pottery came from Athens. It has also been remarked that much of the heavier marble sculpture in this wreck, and indeed in that discovered off Mahdia in 1907, had been made (and probably shipped) in separate pieces with attachments designed for assembly. It is thus reasonable to conjecture that we are dealing with a commercial load on a ship that had left some port, central on the coast of Asia Minor or one of the adjacent Greek islands (my best guess here would be the island of Rhodes), and was traveling westwards through the channel, almost certainly on its way to Italy (presumably the goods being intended for Rome) without first calling at Athens.[5] Several of the minor objects from the wreck are still enigmatic and it is to be hoped that further study of these and perhaps a resumption of underwater archaeology on the site, now that skin-diving has made such progress, will enable the provenance to be ultimately established with greater accuracy. In 1953 some dives were made on the site by divers under Frédéric Dumas in the vessel *Calypso*. He reports that the sponge divers seem to have cleared only the surface of the wreck and that a great deal of the ship remains for future investigators under some 50 centimeters of sand. He also reported,[6] almost incredibly, that there was still paint on the wood of the wreck.

THE DISCOVERY OF THE MECHANISM FRAGMENTS

Strangely enough the mechanism fragments with which we are concerned were not remarked upon until nearly eight months after the excavations had been terminated. With several dozen newspaper and journal accounts of the flow of major and minor objects from Antikythera to the National Museum, there could hardly have been a failure to report the existence of these pieces of corroded bronze with their interesting and clear traces of gear-wheels and with the only extensive, albeit sadly illegible inscription to be found in the wreck. The first account was, however, not published until Friday, 23 May, 1902 (*To Asty*, No. 4141: p. 1) when there appeared the results of an examination of an inscription by the numismatist Svoronos and by the secretary of the Austrian Institute, Wilhelm. The report stated that this inscription had been discovered "last Saturday" (i.e., 17 May, 1902) by the former minister, Staïs. He is said to have found them among the bronze pieces which were kept in a caged enclosure to be examined after the fragments of the great Hermes statue had been joined by the restorers.

Other contemporary news stories make clear the procedure that was being followed. In the museum, the restorers and experts in chemical cleaning were being deluged by an unprecedented motley of bronze and marble fragments. Slowly, all the recognizable pieces were sorted out, tentatively identified, and gradually joined to form more or less complete figures. The formless lumps of scored marble and verdigrised bronze were set on one side to be used later when restoration was more complete. The cage containing the bronze fragments seems to have been in the open, perhaps on the covered portico at the top of the museum steps. Periodically, as the statues grew, these lumps would be examined again and again for clues as to their identity. Doubtless it was on such a search that Staïs suddenly noticed the pieces with inscription.

What is the explanation for this? Can it be that such exciting pieces were accidentally relegated to the stockpile of spare lumps? Theophanidis,[7] writing in 1928, suggests that such formless lumps were broken by the divers and only preserved if they were found thereby to be an object covered in petrified debris rather than a natural lump of discolored rocks. From this one should be led to suppose that the mechanism fragments should have been discovered by the divers but somehow missed by all experts until their sudden late retrieval

---

[4] Peter Cornelis Bol, *Die Skulpturen des Schiffsfundes von Antikythera*, Mitteilungen des deutschen archäologischen Instituts Athenische Abteilung, 2. Beiheft (Gebr. Mann Verlag, Berlin, 1972).

[5] As suggested later (p. 56) there is even a faint but quite unprovable possibility that the ship was carrying the goods of Cicero who had been staying on Rhodes 79 to 77 B.C. and had seen a recently constructed geared planetarium instrument there at the School of Posidonios. I do not know how reasonable it is to think that the statuary from the wreck is such as might have been purchased by a Roman gentleman of taste at this time. Cicero does not mention any loss of his baggage, nor does he write of any relics of this period brought home with him.

[6] Honor Frost, *Under the Mediterranean* (Englewood Cliffs, N. J., Prentice-Hall, 1963), p. 127, n.l.

[7] Jean Théofanidis, "Sur l'instrument en cuivre, dont des fragments se trouvent au Musée Archéologique d'Athènes et qui fut retiré du fond de la mer d'Anticythère en 1902," *Praktika tes Akademias Athenon* **9** (1934): pp. 140–149.

by Staïs. Against this there are several telling reports by the associated archaeologists, commending the divers for their painstaking skill in bringing objects to the surface—even delicate glass vessels, without so much as a trace of recent damage. All breaks were ancient, heavily crusted and patinated.

Now although some surfaces of the mechanism fragments carry such heavy accretions of debris, there are other faces which preserve quite delicate detail and must have been protected during the long underwater period. The conclusion seems clear that the fragments were indeed held together in a formless lump of uninteresting exterior, and that the lump was broken open not by the divers, but at some time shortly before Staïs made his discovery. Now that something is known of the original structure of the mechanism one may make a reasonable conjecture as to why such a lump would suddenly have cracked while resting in its cage outside the museum.

Anticipating this reconstruction, we note that the mechanism was built on a series of bronze plates held together in a wooden frame or case, only tiny fragments of which have been preserved. In the wreck this device was crushed and its corners and part of the outside faces lost, the part remaining then being gradually coated with a hard calcareous deposit at the same time as the metal corroded away to a thin core coated with hard metallic salts preserving much of the former shape of the bronze. When the lump was removed from the ocean and brought to the museum it must have dried slowly from outside to inside through the porous but compact mass.

It is now well known, after several tragic errors, that great care and special treatment are needed to preserve wooden objects excavated from damp sites. If ancient wood dries without special stiffening or replacement of its water, the cell walls collapse and the specimen shrivels miserably into a hard mass distorted in shape and much smaller in bulk. The residue of the wooden case of this mechanism could receive no such treatment and must therefore have shrunk away from its initial position binding together the plates of bronze. Such shrinking would indeed produce cracks to separate the fragments into those four that we have, and everything is consistent with this being the explanation for the most interesting object from the wreck lying unknown to all for months after its retrieval. One must, however, also assume, and it is perhaps not unreasonable to do so, that once the natural cracking had exhibited the fresh surfaces with gears and inscription, further unrecorded cleaning was able to expose some damaged but interesting traces of structure in parts originally near the exterior of the lump. There are no photographs or descriptions of the state of the fragments prior to such initial cleaning as there must have been in May, 1902. There are, however, published accounts and photographs taken between that day and the present, and from these it is possible to follow the progress in cleaning and understanding the fragments.

RESEARCH ON THE MECHANISM FRAGMENTS, 1902–1973

As already stated, the first published account of the discovery of the mechanism appeared in the Athens newspaper *To Asty* (No. 4141, 23 May, 1902). The announcement said that the object had been examined by Svoronos and identified as some sort of astrolabe contained in a box, and that even lines of inscription on it (now lines 15–21, Fragment B reverse) had been partially read by Wilhelm and dated epigraphically to a period extending from about the second century B.C. to the first or second century A.D. On the same day, another article by Svoronos in *Neon Asty* (No. 163: p. 2) claimed that the object was an astrolabe with spherical projections on a set of rings. A couple of days later in *Neon Asty* (No. 165) Konstantin Rados confirmed the inscriptions but noted the great difficulty in reading them, added the opinion that the mechanism looked as if it contained a spring (possibly this was the circular drum of Fragment C), and suggested that, since the statues appeared to be much earlier in date, we had here perhaps a device from a second and later shipwreck.

Within a week of the initial announcement, controversy had broken out and plans were being made for further work. On 29 May (*To Asty*, No. 4147: p. 1) it was noted that the object had been photographed and exhibited on the previous day and that Rados had described it before the Geographical Society, claiming that it was not an astrolabe. It was further stated that Rousopoulos had been asked to attend to the conservation of the fragments. By the next day (*To Asty* 30 May, 1902, No. 4148: p. 1) a committee had been formed and an examination undertaken by Lieutenant Rediadis. He suggested that the object might well be connected with the astrolabe described by Philoponus (Alexandria, *ca.* 625 A.D.) and thus joined forces with Svoronos against Rados who still maintained, quite correctly, that the object seemed too complex for any type of traditional astrolabe. The debate continued with an alignment of experts for and against the astrolabe identification, and apparently some difference of opinion as to the extent of the cleaning to be conducted by Rousopoulos.

The first flurry of excitement was now superseded by the more deliberate process of scholarly publication. A first full account of the Antikythera treasure in general was published during the year in *Ephemeris* (1902), but of the seven plates only one gives detail of the mechanism; the part reproduced is of the inscription of Fragment B reverse, identical with the definitive 1908 publication by Svoronos, probably issued separately already in 1903. With the lapse of the next few years there was comparatively little progress of description or analysis. In 1905 Rados presented his views on the mechanism at the International Archaeological Congress in Athens (*Comptes Rendues,* 1905: pp. 256–258) and Staïs retold his in a booklet, *Peri ton Antikytheron Eurematon* (Athens, 1905), which more narrowly dates the wreck as first century B.C.

Shortly after this there seems to have entered the arena the great classical philologist, Albert Rehm of Munich, to whom much of the later technical elucidation of the fragments is due. His first publication on the subject (*Philologische Wochenschrift,* 1907: cols. 467–470) consists of a review of the paper presented by Rediadis in 1907 which is identical with that reproduced in the definitive publication of the Antikythera treasure by Svoronos 1902–1908. His review is justifiably most critical of the lack of detail given in the text and of the hopelessly inadequate photographic reproductions of the fragments. From his firsthand examination of the fragments, he observes the complicated gearing and concludes with Rados and against Svoronos that the object cannot possibly have been any sort of astrolabe. Also at this time, as reported by other writers, Rehm seems to have been able to read (on the main front dial of the instrument on Fragment C1) at a place previously covered, the month name ΠΑΧΩΝ (Pachon) which is used in the Greek forms of both the Egyptian (rotating) and the Alexandrian (fixed) calendars. Rehm concluded from the appearance of this name that the machine must be subsequent to the Julian calendar reform of 46 B.C. which added the intercalary days in leap years and thereby gave rise to the Alexandrian form of reckoning. In fact the name occurs on a ring which is movable to permit it to represent the rotation of the Egyptian calendar rather than the Alexandrian, and the argument loses all validity since the Egyptian style occurs already in Plato and was preserved long after the Julian reform, for example by Ptolemy, for all astronomical calculation where its regularity makes it most convenient.

Rehm's review was answered at length by Rediadis in *Ephemeris* (Athens, 1910) 3: cols. 157–172. He notes that, if the device was no astrolabe, then it was also clearly not to be identified with a planetarium device like the "Sphere of Archimedes" which had been proposed by Rehm: the fragments showed the mechanism to be too big, too weak, and too flat for such an interpretation, and, in any case, there was absolutely nothing to show that waterpower had been used to drive it. Rediadis stood his ground, adding that, since the object was found on the ship and was originally, he supposes, in a wooden case about 40 centimeters square, it might well be some sort of navigation instrument. This article also contains an interesting chemical analysis of the metal fragments that had been made by Damberge; it showed the material to be copper containing about 4.1 per cent of tin and no other metals in quantity. In other words the device was quite certainly made of bronze rather than brass, a copper-zinc alloy.

Rehm appears to have worked on the fragments spasmodically for several decades after this, intending an eventual publication when the material had fallen into sufficient order. Unfortunately, this was not achieved before his death, and his valuable notes and photographs lay unpublished. I am grateful to Dr. Karl Dachs, of the Bayerische Staatsbibliothek at Munich, to that institution, and to the widow of Professor Rehm for making this material available to me for the present studies. The photographs from this corpus were particularly valuable for they showed the fragments in a state prior to several cleanings which have revealed new areas and much more detail, but also have necessarily destroyed some of the old evidence.

In the absence of Rehm's monograph, work proceeded slowly for many years and on a basis of little more than the material already published by Svoronos. Such indeed were the accounts given by Constantine Rados, *Peri ton Thesauron ton Antikytheron* (Athens, 1910), by Hermann Diels, *Antike Teknik* (2nd ed., Leipzig and Berlin, 1920), p. 28, n. 1, and by A. Schlachter, "Der Globus," *Stoicheia* 8 (Berlin, 1927): pp. 53–54. A new set of photographs of the fragments was taken by the National Archaeological Museum in 1918 (the negatives are dated IX 13/18) and these show extra detail revealed after a new cleaning; these photographs were published by Ernst Zinner, *Geschichte der Sternkunde* (Berlin, 1931), p. 111, where the instrument is referred to the time of Christ, and by Robert T. Gunther, *Astrolabes of the World* (Oxford, 1932) 1: pp. 55–58, pl. 26, figs. 53–57, where it is dated (for no apparent reason) *ca.* 250 A.D.

The only major investigation of the fragments before the present work seems to have been that started by Rear-Admiral Jean Theophanidis in 1928 in connection with the preparation of an article on the voyages of St. Paul in the *Great Military and Nautical Encyclopaedia* (1: pp. 83–96). This work was presented in fuller form in two articles published in conjunction with a third by K. Maltezos in *Praktika tes Akademias Athenon* 9 (Athens 1934): pp. 140–153. Maltezos gives only a general summary of the prior literature, but Theophanidis adds much new information about the gearing visible on the fragments and proposes reconstructions which involve stereographic projection and raise once more the question of identifying the instrument with an astrolabe. Unfortunately in the short space of this article there was not room for any complete and systematic reconstruction of the fragments and their mechanism and it is not completely clear how such hypothetical and tentative findings are related to the evidence.

Of more recent literature before the present work there in only repetition of the material already summarized. Willy Hartner in Arthur U. Pope, *A Survey* of *Persian Art* (Oxford 1939) **3**: p. 2531, n. 3, gives an excellent short account, but is unduly influenced by the claims of Theophanidis for the existence of evidence that stereographic projection was used in laying out the circles of the instrument. Zinner, *Entstehung und Ausbreitung des Coppernicanischen Lehre* (Erlangen, 1943) repeats his earlier mentions and publishes the new photographs, and George Karo, "Art Salvaged from the Sea," *Archaeology* **1** (1948): pp. 179–185, gives a very fine general account of the Antikythera wreck and its companion pieces of underwater archaeology.

From about 1951, in the course of investigations into the history of scientific instruments with special reference to ancient astrolabes and planetaria, I began to appreciate the deep significance of the Antikythera mechanism which was known to me through the writings of Gunther, Svoronos, and Zinner. The director of the National Archaeological Museum of Athens, Dr. Christos Karouzos was most cooperative in providing me in 1953 with a new and much clearer set of photographs than any that had been published, and from these it became evident very quickly that the work of cleaning had proceeded since the time of Rehm so that fresh detail was evident, but that the complication was so great that only first-hand examination could enable this detail to be related to the structure of the original device. On the basis of the photographs, I published a new evaluation of the Antikythera mechanism in an article, "Clockwork before the Clock," *Horological Journal* (5 October, 1955, in numbers for December, 1955, and January, 1956) which was reprinted in several languages and also summarized in an article in *A History of Technology,* ed. Singer, Holmyard and Hall (Oxford, 1957), **3**: p. 618, fig. 364.

In the summer of 1958, aided by a grant from the American Philosophical Society, I had the privilege of examing the fragments in Athens, being given all facilities there by the museum, and having in addition the help of a most competent epigrapher, Dr. George Stamires, then my colleague at the Institute for Advanced Study, Princeton, New Jersey. The original publication by Svoronos had noted only 220 letters of the inscriptions; Theophanidis was able to extend this to about 350 letters; Stamires read eventually some 793 letters in all.

On my return I was able to publish fairly rapidly a preliminary reconstruction and analysis of the mechanism, "An Ancient Greek Computer," *Scientific American* (June, 1959), pp. 60 ff., and to include some consideration of it in a previously written, more extensive monograph, "On the Origin of Clockwork, Perpetual Motion Devices and the Compass," *United States National Museum Bulletin* **218** (Washington, D. C., 1959).

These publications, particularly the former, gave rise to a great deal of public attention, scholarly and otherwise. Among the accounts in the Athens press was a wild claim by an American professor emeritus that I had been fooled by the apparent antiquity of the device and that it was in fact a modern intrusion on the wreck and merely a planetarium or orrery of the type with which he had been taught the elements of the Copernican system in an Austrian school some sixty years before (*Kathimerini,* January 8, 1959). I must confess that many times in the course of these investigations I have awakened in the night and wondered whether there was some way round the evidence of the texts, the epigraphy, the style of construction and the astronomical content, all of which point very firmly to the first century B.C. There is also the fact that it is all made of bronze rather than the brass which has been used for most scientific instruments since the late Middle Ages.

Then again there were some only too ready to believe that the complexity of the device and its mechanical sophistication put it so far beyond the scope of Hellenistic technology that it could only have been designed and created by alien astronauts coming from outer space and visiting our civilization. Needless to say—or perhaps it is not—though I sympathize with the shock one may feel at revising upwards the estimation of Hellenistic technology, I cannot agree with any so radical interpretation. I feel rather that the whole story of Greek science makes a great deal more sense if we assume that the old view of their rising no higher than the simple Heronic devices was a drastic underestimation that can now be corrected.

After two years of attempted reconstruction, I was ready to check joins identified from the previous measurements, and in June, 1961, assisted by a grant from the American Council of Learned Societies, I revisited Athens and was once more permitted to work with the fragments themselves, checking inscriptions and joins for a final reconstruction. The joins were quite successful, but even with them it was disappointing to find that there was still neither enough visible of the gearing or of the dial work to make any much more certain interpretation possible of the working of the device. I attempted to make a statement for the cooperative re-examination of the wreck that was edited by Gladys Weinberg in 1965, but realized then that not very much could be added to the accounts I had already published.

Though I continued to work at the puzzle of the fragments during the next several years it was not until 1971 that a major breakthrough presented itself. In that year I was alerted by a new publication [8] to the possibility of using gamma-radiography to see through the corrosion and accretion of the fragments. I had long before asked the authorities of the Greek National Museum whether an x-ray investigation would be in order, but no such equipment had been available and

---

[8] F. J. Miller, E. V. Sayre and B. Keisch, *Isotopic Methods of Examination and Authentication in Art and Archaeology,* Oak Ridge National Laboratory IIC-21 (Oak Ridge, October, 1970).

in any case there would be difficulties of supplying heavy electrical power within the museum. Now, through the courtesy of Dr. Alvin Weinberg of Oak Ridge National Laboratories and of Dr. A. F. Rupp of the Isotopes Development Center, I was put in touch with the authorities of the Greek Atomic Energy Commission, and received from them immediately the most cordial cooperation.[9] I also had the good fortune to be put in touch, through their offices with Dr. Ch. Karakalos who undertook the painstaking work of preparing first the gamma-radiographs and then a series of fine x-radiographs, a labor that entailed long exposures, delicate positioning of the fragments, and much preliminary analysis of the plates so that exposures could be adjusted to reveal the important detail even though the specimens were extremely non-uniform in their radiographic transparencies. I also must specially acknowledge the work of Mrs. Emily Karakalos who assisted her husband in making the all-important counts of gear teeth, a task that is delicate, tedious, and subject to maddening errors and repetitions before consistent results can be obtained.

Being on sabbatical leave in Europe during 1972, and with the assistance of a research grant from the National Science Foundation (GS 28993), I was able to visit twice with Dr. Karakalos and go through the radiographs. It was evident from the beginning that so much of the gearing was preserved within the fragments, and so clear was the detail that much more of the form and structure of the gear trains could be elucidated. Bit by bit Karakalos and I were able to analyze the crucial cases where meshing between certain wheels was doubtful. We examined very carefully the structure of the differential turntable and of the gearing of the lower back dial and established their connections with little doubt and to such accuracy that for the first time the gear ratios could be associated with well-known astronomical and calendrical parameters.

In all it was a most exciting sudden advance in the solving of the puzzle, and there was a certain romantic justness to the cooperation between the fine modern physical facilities of the Greek Atomic Energy Commission, the directors and authorities [10] of the Greek National Museum, and ourselves in this attempt to throw light on what was now clearly one of the most important pieces of evidence for the understanding of ancient Greek science and technology. Finally, as most of the rest of the gear train mechanism had fallen into place leaving only the system around the upper back dial incomplete there was rediscovered in the museum store the long-lost Fragment D which had been available to me only from photographs. This was now quickly radiographed by Karakalos in June, 1973, and proved to be almost certainly the missing link that was needed for this section. Thus it turned out that the greater part of the gearing system was a complete entity and though many puzzles remain, it was possible to prepare a definitive account of the results achieved.

As will be shown in the technical analysis which follows, the mechanism can now be identified as a calendrical Sun and Moon computing mechanism which may have been made about 87 B.C. and used for a couple of years during which time it had several repairs. It was perhaps made by a mechanician associated with the school of Posidonios on the island of Rhodes and may have been wrecked while being shipped to Rome about the time that Cicero was visiting that school ca. 78 B.C. The design of the mechanism seems to be very much in the tradition that began with the design of planetarium devices by Archimedes. It was continued through the Rhodian activity, transmitted to Islam where similar geared devices were produced, and finally flowered in the European Middle Ages with the tradition of great astronomical clocks and related mechanical devices which were crucial for the Scientific and Industrial Revolutions. Perhaps the most spectacular aspect of the mechanism is that it incorporates the very sophisticated device of a differential gear assembly for taking the difference between two rotations, and one must now suppose that such complex gearing is more typical of the level of Greco-Roman mechanical proficiency than has been thought on the basis of merely textual evidence. Thus this singular artifact, the oldest existing relic of scientific technology, and the only complicated mechanical device we have from antiquity quite changes our ideas about the Greeks and makes visible a more continuous historical evolution of one of the most important main lines that lead to our modern civilization.

THE CASING, GENERAL CONSTRUCTION, AND DIAL WORK

JOINS OF THE FRAGMENTS

Although it was not apparent to the earlier workers, nor indeed to me before the structure of the four extant fragments had been clarified, all four pieces form physical joins which show that originally they were part of a single mass (see fig. 6). Fragment C covers the lower left corner of the front of the main Fragment A, Fragment B covers the top right of the back of Fragment A, and Fragment D fits between B and A at the center of the annular rings of the dial plate of B.

In the original state as found I think that debris similar to that on top of C.1 covered much of the lower portion of the main drive wheel on the front of Fragment A, much more such cover can be seen on the older photographs in which Fragment C seems much more extensive prior to cleaning, and this together with the accretions directly over the rest of the front surface of Fragment A could have left little visible trace of the

---

[9] I would like to accord my thanks for this to General Demopoulos, Dr. G. Fragatos, and Dr. D. A. Kappos, who served as directors during the period of this research.

[10] I would like to direct special thanks to Director Kallipolitis, Dr. N. Yalouris, and to all the museum staff for their most helpful and kind consideration to me and to Dr. Karakalos.

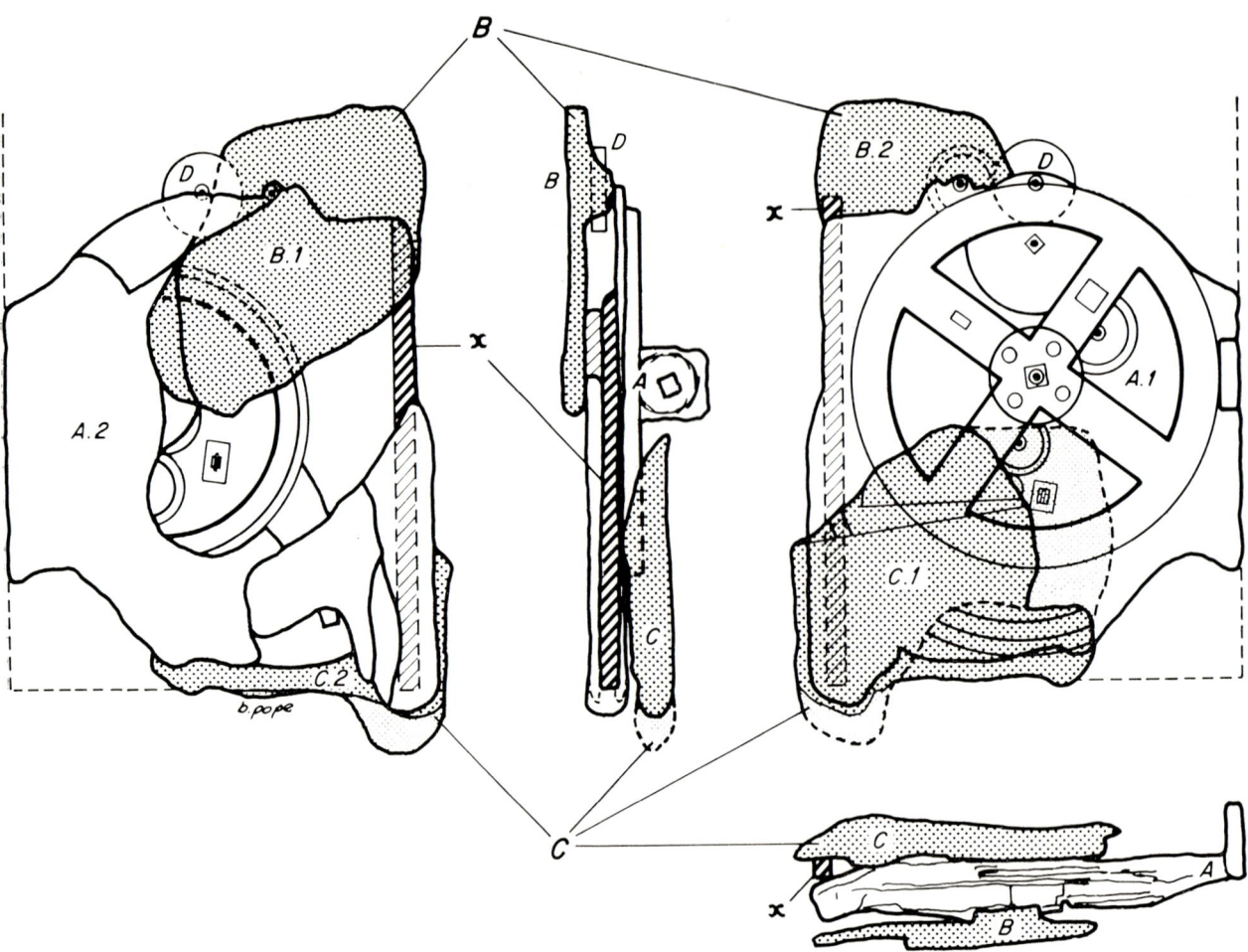

Fig. 6. Schematic diagram showing the joins of the four main fragments. The wooden member whose shrinking may have provoked the splitting apart of the original mass is shown at x.

underlying mechanism. On the back surface of Fragment A there must have been a fairly complete layer of debris which extended from the section preserved as Fragment B all the way down to the part of the lower back dial that is preserved at the lower right corner of the back of Fragment A. I suppose that the inscribed sheet which made mirror image impressions on both Fragments A and B and is preserved now only in a tiny piece must have been much more extensive and perhaps fell off and was mislaid only after recovery.

Along the right-hand margin of the back and the lower left-hand corner of the front of the main Fragment A there occur small pieces of a brownish rock-like substance adhering to what seems to be the remains of a sort of channel. Though the mechanical details are difficult to see, I take this to be the traces of what were once the wooden side walls of the casing of the instrument. Rediadis and Rehm both refer to a wooden casing, so possibly it was more visible then or there existed other fragments of it before my examinations.

Visible in the radiographs at the corner of Fragment C is a small object which may be a fixing bracket or more probably a sliding locator pin by which the front dial plate could be fixed to the side wall so as to be removable for access to the mechanism. Along the long surviving side of Fragment A the radiographs show clearly a shadow of the channel running the entire length.

THE BACK DIALS

The fitting together of the four fragments is attested both by physical fit and color match on the one hand and by the structure of the dial work on the other. Fragment C provides a concentric pair of dials which seem to fit around the outer perimeter of the main drive wheel, and Fragment B provides a set of concentric dials which would fall directly above and match the very similar set preserved on the lower part of the back of the mechanism. Each of these dials consists of a central plate of 44.3 mm radius surrounded by a series of annuli each of average width 5.92 mm separated from each other by gaps of average width 1.35 mm.

For the upper dial which is preserved in Fragment B, I count four such complete rings; reading from the center plate to the outer limb the radii being 44.3, 45.8, 53.0, 53.8, 59.1, 60.4, 65.9, 67.7, and 73.4 mm. Just within the center plate, the width of an annulus inside the perimeter, there is a short segment of what appears to be another gap, but I take this to be more probably an accidental cut or crack than some sort of additional partial ring. The rings are partly held in place by a special bridge which straddles them below the dial surface. It consists of a strip which is rivetted to the center plate and the outside limb; it has a width of 3–4 mm and a height of 3 mm. On top of the fragment of dial plate, in a radial position, but much obscured by surrounding debris is an object that might perhaps be the one preserved portion of a dial pointer. It consists of a long thin bar of length 55 mm, thickness 2.5 mm, and width 4.5 mm. The length is clearly not sufficient to extend from the dial center to the outside limb, but it might have been broken; there are no recognizable features visible to the naked eye or the radiography.

The lower back dial which is preserved at the bottom right hand corner of the back of the main Fragment A has also a center plate of identical radius, 44.3 mm. On the radiograph the inner two surrounding annuli are quite clear and I measure the successive radii, reading outwards as before, as 44.3, 45.8, 52.3, and 53.4 mm. Beyond this is a third annulus, somewhat displaced from its original position, but evidently of the same general width and spacing. Beyond this again it is just possible that there may be a fourth annulus as in the upper back dial, but I cannot clearly discern any trace of it by eye or from the radiographs. Though the entire dial is much distorted at this point I fancy that the width of the engraved and inscribed fixed limb around this dial at this point does not leave enough room for a fourth annulus. I therefore suppose this dial to have only three such annuli together with a fixed outer limb. Neither in this dial nor the upper one is the fixed center plate inscribed with scale. The only markings on them are the small subsidiary dials. The annuli of the lower dial are also held together by a bridge, visible to the naked eye and the radiographs. It is very similar in dimensions to that on the upper dial, but in this case one can see from the end-on view that it consists of a series of U-shaped sections, U-U-U, presumably to straddle the gaps between the annuli and allow them to be turned freely.

The upper dial therefore seems to consist of a central plate with subsidiary dial, and four rotatable annuli. The lower dial probably has only three rotatable annuli, but in this the fixed outer limb is divided also. One cannot tell whether or not the upper dial also had a fixed outer limb. The upper dial is in a much corroded state, heavily accreted so that all divisions and inscriptions are extremely difficult to see, and quite unintelligible, but the general impression is that it is heavily inscribed and might one day be more readable after further cleaning. Along the radius passing through the center of the subsidiary dial I think I see a continuous line of graduations running across all the visible annuli, and on the outermost of the annuli I see, somewhat uncertainly, a stretch of five even graduations subtending in all about 38° of arc. By calculation this would yield some 47 or 48 graduations around the entire circle. For the lower dial there are problems of locating the center since the inner disc has been displaced with respect to the outer limb on which quite clear graduation marks are to be seen. I measure again five such divisions and find they subtend just a little more than 30°, say approximately 31° which would give a count of 58 such divisions in the circle. The accuracy is such that a count of 59 (half days in the synodic month) is by no means excluded. Unlike the upper dial, the lower has comparatively little inscription, only a small proportion of the divisions being annotated. For what is legible of the inscriptions see p. 48, fig. 37.

The two back dials are so large that between them they must virtually fill the entire back face of the instrument. The fourth annulus of the upper dial has an outer radius of 73.4 mm and therefore even without any outer limb its diameter would almost fill the approximately 150.0 mm width measured across the main plate of the instrument. If the lower dial has, as I believe, three annuli and a fixed and engraved outer limb it would be of about the same diameter as the upper dial, but in this case we know from the small preserved fragment that the dial plate extends about 6.0 mm beyond and to the right of the outer scale on the limb. It would seem that the dial plate overhangs by this amount a wooden side wall of about 6.0 mm thickness which surrounds the preserved main dial plate. The back dial plate must therefore be about 158.0 mm wide. I suggest that in fact the dimension was determined as just 8 digits (i.e. half a Roman foot) in width with an additional overhang of about a quarter of a digit on either side.

The distance BG between the central Axis B of the main drive wheel, and the center G of the lower dial is 78.0 mm and this leaves as much margin between the outer limb and the center line through B as there is in the overhang at the sides. A similar overhang at the lower edge would imply that the back dial plate extends to about 158.0 mm below Axis B, so that the dial is inscribed within a square that constitutes the lower half of this back plate.

One might expect that the upper back dial would be located in a similar fashion, but such apparently is not quite the case. The center of the upper dial, Axis N, appears to be located just beyond the top of the periphery of the main drive wheel at a distance $BN = 63.0$ mm from Axis B. The distance between the two dial centers is therefore $GN = 141.0$ mm which is less than the sum of the two equal dial radii by a deficit of

$2(73.4) - 141.0 = 5.8$ mm. If the dials were to be arranged to touch without overlapping we would have to assume that the upper dial were centered on an Axis N' situated 5.8 mm further from Axis B which would bring it almost to the perimeter of the Wheel $M1$. This in turn would require that the tooth counts of the Pinion $M2$ and the Wheel N should sum to the 96 teeth of $M1$; the Wheel N' in this location should therefore have *ca.* 80 teeth rather than the 64 found for Wheel N in Fragment D. Alternatively, noting that the amount of deficit is exactly that of one annulus of either the upper or the lower dial, one could satisfy the demand for neatness by supposing that the upper dial has four annuli and the lower three, and that neither has an engraved outer limb, at least not in the region where they would intersect.

Symmetry could be complete by different means if the Axis N were moved still further out to a place N'' such that $BN'' = BG = 79.3$ mm, but this places N'' at a distance of 32.9 mm beyond Axis M and would require a wheel on this axis having about 116 teeth to engage with the Pinion $M2$. I find the question almost impossible to resolve with the present evidence alone. The gearing behind the upper back dial is the most uncertain part of the entire train system in the mechanism, and the deformation which has occurred at the join of this Fragment B to the main Fragment A is larger than anywhere else. Furthermore one cannot rely too heavily on small differences between large interaxial distances when the axes themselves are so difficult to locate. In all I feel it is safest to assume that the Fragment D fits here and that the upper dial is located in a slightly assymmetrical position to fit the axis positions determined by the requirements of the gearing.

At all events, the total height of the back plate must have been such that it would contain approximately four dial radii of 73.4 mm each and overhangs top and bottom of about 6.0 mm each giving a total of 305.6 mm. I suggest, as before, that the intention here was a length of just 16 digits (one Roman foot) with an additional overhang of about a quarter of a digit on either side. The back dial plate therefore must have had dimensions of about one foot by half a foot, surrounded by overhangs to cover the wooden sides and almost completely occupied by the upper and lower dials. From the evidence of the small, partly legible but almost unintelligible fragment of inscription preserved it seems that the space between the dials to the right of center contained a short text. Probably that to the left contained a similar text each of them having perhaps thirty lines at the most.

In addition to this it can be seen from the extensive mirror image inscriptions in the regions of the upper and lower dials and from the small fragments which still exist of the plate, inscribed side facing the dials, that the entire area was covered by a plate containing a quite long text of at least 47 lines. It seems that this text referred to the general calendric cycles which were embodied in the geared mechanism and I think it clear that this plate must have served as a hinged door or more probably pair of doors hinged so as to cover and protect the dial system.

THE FRONT DIAL

The front dial plate is attested only by Fragment C which contains two annuli, rather similar to and of the same width as those on the back dials, but fortunately in a much better state of preservation. The inner radius is 62.5 mm. The middle radius is 70.0 mm and the outer radius is 77.2 mm which shows that the overall diameter is only a shade smaller than the total dial plate width of 158.0 mm, leaving a margin of only about 1.9 mm on either side. What is more, it seems from a straight boundary at the lower edge of the fragment that the dial plate was inscribed within a square of side 158.0 mm so that additional plates would be needed to cover a casing large enough to surround the main plate of the mechanism which extends to what seems, especially from the older photographs, like a clear lower edge about 104.0 mm below the level of the main Axis B. Although the present physical join of Fragments A and C makes their lower edges nearly agree, it is clear that there has been a large deformation at this point, probably because the dial plate was originally held high above the main plate surface. If the dial plate were in its presumably correct position, centered on Axis B, its lower edge would be about 25.0 mm above the lower edge of the main plate.

If one supposes the entire front of the instrument were covered by a dial plate the same size as that at the back, and that only the center of this were occupied by a square plate containing the single dial it would leave rectangular plates above and below. These would be each about 158.0 mm wide and 79.0 mm high. Now the parapegma inscription which adheres to Fragment C and carries a legend referring to the scales on this dial is a little less than 80.0 mm wide, and a height of 79.0 mm of such a plate would contain just about fourteen lines of inscription, a little more than half the Greek alphabet of twenty-four letters. It would therefore seem that two columns of such text, each about 79.0 mm square could carry the entire set of key letters. For this reason one might suggest that the front plate was extended in this way, either in the form of a single sheet which has accidentally broken exactly at the boundary of the parapegma inscription, or more probably in three separate sheets, an upper one which might well have been the main dedicatory inscription of the instrument, a middle dial plate, and a lower parapegma plate.

The only difficulty with the above explanation is that the present parapegma plate seems to terminate with a straight edge below the line for letter Σ which is the eighteenth in the alphabet. It is, of course, quite possible that the first five or six letters of the alphabet

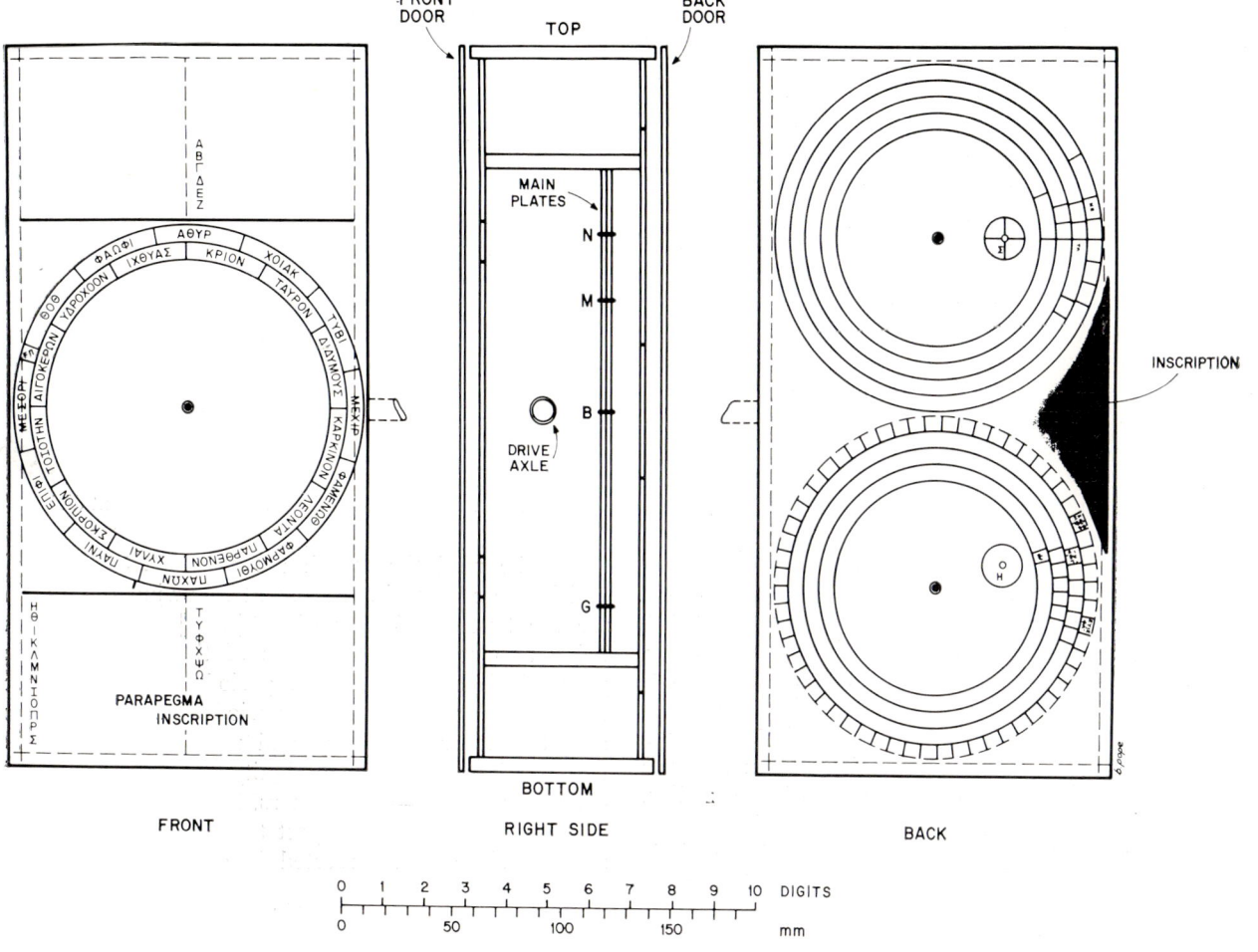

Fig. 7. Reconstruction of the dial plates and casing.

were on the upper plate after an introductory inscription of some sort, followed by the present column which would then have contained twelve letters in the left column, and succeeded by the right hand column containing the remaining six letters of the alphabet followed by a blank space or some concluding text. The small parapegma Fragment iv might then be identified as the top left edge of the lower plate, and Fragments ii and iii might be from the top of its second column which is now squashed upside down below the visible parapegma fragment. The entire parapegma plate appears to have been twisted and folded so that the part now visible is upside down but in almost the correct location.

The front dial itself is so arranged that the inner annulus is immovably fixed in position and held in place by a channel-shaped support under it connecting it to the limb. The outer annulus between it and the limb is capable of rotation in the same manner as those of the back dials. An interesting difference, invisible to the naked eye, can be seen from the radiographs. The gap between the two annuli is not blank but contains a series of tiny holes, one per degree. From their position it is difficult to tell whether they lie near the outer boundary of the inner annulus or the inner boundary of the outer one, most probably the latter. I suppose these holes to have been made for the insertion of a marker which could be moved from day to day (as with a traditional parapegma calendar) to show the current place in the year.

Both inner and outer annuli are graduated with short marks at degree intervals, and longer marks across the entire band every 30°. The inner (fixed) annulus is evidently still in its original position for one of the long marks occurs exactly along the mid-line of the dial face. The entire 30° segment clockwise from this division is in a good state of preservation and at its center can be read the name ΧΥΛΑΙ (Chelai, the Claws of the Scorpion—i.e., the zodiacal sign Libra). In the preceding segment one can just make out the two letters of [ΠΑΡΘΕ]ΝΟ[Υ] (Virgo) so confirming that we have the cycle of the zodiac proceeding clockwise and beginning with Libra at the lower limb. This is somewhat unexpected for the traditional orientation of the zodiac circle on later instruments and horoscopes, though also using the clockwise sense, places the equinoxes to left and right and the solstices on the upper and lower limbs, usually with the summer solstice high and the winter low. It is, of course, possible that the jumbling of fragments has been even more serious than here supposed and that the extant fragment belongs to one of the other corners of the dial plate.

Straddling the first degree division of Libra, just above the top of the pair of short graduating marks I read plainly the letter A. Not nearly so clearly, but with some considerable doubt, I think I see spanning the 11th, 14th and 16th degrees of the same sign the letters B, Γ and Δ respectively, and even more uncertainly, above the marks of the first degree of the next sign (Scorpio) an E. In Virgo, also with great uncertainty I think that at the 18th degree may be read an Ω. These letters of the alphabet inscribed in order along the zodiac, apparently beginning and ending with the autumnal equinox are without much doubt to be linked one by one with the lines of the parapegma text. As the Sun enters each marked degree of the zodiac, the parapegma calendar tells the heliacal risings and settings of the most noticeable bright stars. This is exactly the tradition of Greek astronomical calendars of the period, but further identification is difficult since we do not, alas, have the parapegma inscription and the marking letters from the same part of the zodiac. Those of the extant text all refer to events just before the summer solstice, just three-quarters of the circle and of the calendar away from the preserved parts of the divided circles.

The major division of the outer annulus are a little more than half a sign out of phase with the zodiac scale; a major division occurring at the mark of the 17th degree of Libra. At the center of the segment preceding this division, just above the mark A at Libra

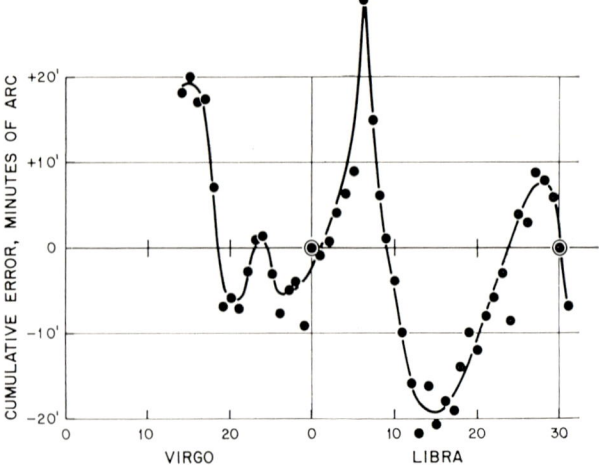

FIG. 9. Error of graduation of divisions on front dial.

1, can be read the month name ΠΑΧΩΝ (Pachon), and in the center of the segment following the division are the first two letters of ΠΑ[ΥΝΙ] (Payni), these being two consecutive months of the Greco-Egyptian year which consisted of 12 periods of 30 days each followed by an epagomenal period of 5 days with no adjustment for leap years and no irregularities. Because of its absolute unambiguity this calendar was in common use by all astronomers, but it had the property of a steady drift with respect to the solar year and its seasons, since this, corrected in our calendar by leap years, is almost a quarter day longer than the 365 days of this cycle. Each return to the same place in the zodiac will therefore take a quarter day more than the cycle of the months and the outer annulus must correspondingly be moved anticlockwise through a quarter division. In the present setting Libra 0° corresponds with 13½ Pachon, and 30 Pachon = 0 Payni with the mark of Libra 17°. Thus 13½ divisions on the month scale correspond to 13° on the zodiac scale though the difference between the scales of 365 days and 360° should only be about a third of this half day. Clearly non-uniform division, probably of both scales, and probably unintentional, is the reason. At all events the approximate alignment of the autumnal equinox with 13½ Pachon is clear.[11]

Since, as just noted, the cycle of months moves with respect to the solar year at the rate of a quarter day every year it should be possible to use this alignment to date the position recorded by the instrument if this

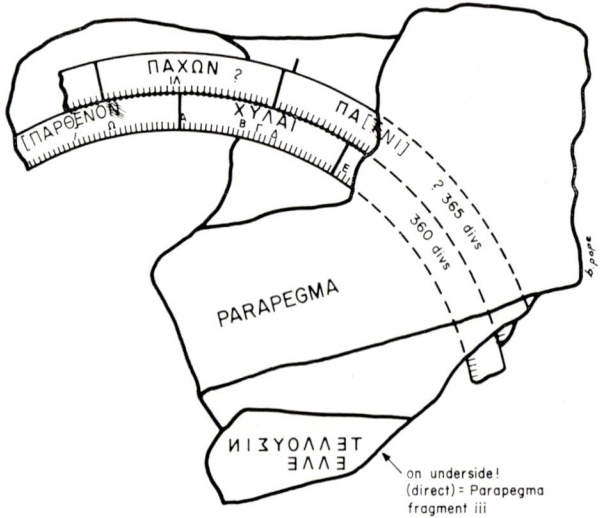

FIG. 8. Front dial fragment.

---

[11] A further ambiguity is due to the fact that one cannot be sure in the case of these instrumental divisions whether the dividing line between Virgo and Libra, and therefore the equinox is to be called Virgo 30° = Libra 0° or (the beginning of) Libra 1°. From the fact that the key letters for the parapegma straddle the degree divisions, I suspect that it is the intervals rather than the divisions which were numbered. The equinox is therefore probably referred to as (the beginning of) Libra 1° and should straddle that interval.

is in a place where it was set intentionally and has not moved since. Before that consideration, however, it is worth remarking that just beyond the outer annulus, just half a division to the right of the long dividing line between Pachon and Payni there is a short but clear incised line—I feel sure it is no accidental crack. I think that this mark, near the lower edge of the front dial, is in fact a fiducial mark which was inscribed at the date of manufacture of the instrument giving the position of the month circle at that time. The half-day displacement from the present position so that Libra 0° corresponds to the 13th day of a month would therefore correspond to a present setting just two years later than that date.

Now it is attested from the *Almagest* of Ptolemy that the autumnal equinox at the time of Hipparchus, in 147 B.C. was on the 3rd Epagomenal day, and that 285 years later, by Ptolemy's own observation it had moved forward to the 9th Athyr. In 87 B.C. it was therefore at the 13th Thoth and two years later, in 85 B.C. it was at the 13½ Thoth. At multiples of 120 years before and after these dates other months would have had their 13th and 13½th days coinciding with the autumnal equinox. For the month of Pachon to come round, however, would take 8 months worth of these quarter-day additions and therefore correspond to a date *ca*. 876 A.D. or 586 B.C. both of which are beyond the range of archaeological possibility.

The evidence therefore of the fiducial mark is that the instrument was engraved *ca* 87 B.C. or at some other date distant from that by a multiple of 120 years, 34 A.D., 154 A.D., etc. For the first possibility the month set by the autumnal equinox would have been Thoth, for the other choices it would have been Phaophi and Athyr respectively. For dates earlier, the five epagomanal days intervene, and the corresponding date in the month Mesori would correspond to 230 B.C.

The evidence from the setting of the month Pachon on the annulus is difficult to evaluate. One possibility is simply that the ring was moved carelessly or accidentally to a quite incorrect position. Another pos-

TABLE 1

ACCURACY OF DIVISION OF THE ZODIAC SCALE ON FRONT DIAL

Number of degree division	Size in tenths of a mm
Vigro	
15	34
16	31
17	33
18	27
19	24
20	34
21	32
22	35
23	35
24	33
25	30
26	30
27	34
28	33
29	30
30	38
Libra	
1	32
2	32
3	34
4	34
5	34
6	34
7	44
8	25
9	28
10	30
11	30
12	30
13	30
14	28
15	37
16	28
17	35
18	32
19	35
20	35
21	32
22	36
23	34
24	34
25	30
26	38
27	32
28	36
29	32
30	32
Scorpio	
1	29

TABLE 2

DISTRIBUTION

Size of degree division, tenths of a mm	Number of such divisions
24	1
25	1
26	0
27	1
28	3
29	1
30	8
31	1
32	8
33	3
34	9
35	5
36	2
37	1
38	2
⋮	⋮
44	1
Total	47 divisions
Arithmetic mean	3.245 mms/division

sibility is that the dial system was marked, not by a single pointer marking both the zodiac and month scales, but by a pair of pointers out of phase by exactly 120°—perhaps there was a complicated structure within this dial place forcing some such arrangement. If for this reason or any other we suppose the outer annular month scale to be set correctly in date though not with a possible month, we could say that such a setting corresponded with a date about two years after that indicated by the fiducial mark. One would have therefore a period of use that would accord well with the finding that the mechanism has been broken and mended in a couple of places, but must have broken down rather quickly in view of the tremendous complication and friction of the gearing system.

Though the dating is of great importance I see no more reasonable way of escaping from the fact that the Sign Libra and the Month Pachon seem to be incorrectly juxtaposed by exactly 120°. Both readings seem quite secure and there seems no room for alternative explanation.

Because the divided circles of this front dial are the only scientifically divided scales that have come down to us from antiquity I have thought it worth while to investigate more fully the accuracy of this division. From an enlarged photograph (times 2.6) of the scales, micrometric readings were taken of the width of each degree mark over the available 46° of well-defined detail. The average size of a degree interval at this magnification was 3.217 mm and the standard deviation was 0.325 mm corresponding to an accuracy of ± 6 minutes of arc. From a cumulated graph of the deviation from average length, it was found that assuming the ends of Libra had been correctly positioned the maximum deviation elsewhere from true amounted to nearly half a degree or about five standard deviations (see table 1 and fig. 2).

Affixed by corrosion beneath the corner of the front dial section and its overlaying parapegma plates is an interesting drumlike component. It consists of a cylindrical drum 30.4 mm in radius built upon a disc 26.0 mm in radius and having an outer wall about 3.6 mm in thickness and 7–8 mm high. Near the outer perimeter of the disc, in the direction of the corner of the dial plate is a small hole of radius 2.3 mm and between this and the center of the disc are the remains of what seems to be a small sliding bracket. On the disc there are also traces of an eccentric circular band about half the size of the disc. At the center of the disc is a squared hole of about 3 mm across with is sides oriented about 22° out of line with the hole and bracket. By the side of the hole is an inscribed letter T. I believe it to be the same letter noted by Theophanidis as a Γ, but I see clear traces of the serif of the left hand bar.

It is difficult to interpret the function of this piece. From its position it might be some part of the dial work for the center of the front dial, possibly a plate indicating the position of the Moon and turned by the inner axle at Axis B. Alternatively, from its construction it is possible that it may be a crank handle designed to fit over the missing shaft that drives the contrate Wheel A. If so the bracket device and the hole may be the remains of a folding handle. Such a cranklike device mounted on a disc would be quite remarkable [12] for the period but in the context of this extraordinary complexity the possibility exists.

THE ARRANGEMENT IN DEPTH OF THE PLATES AND COMPONENTS OF THE MECHANISM

From all the surviving fragments it appears that the entire assembly and almost all the components were built from bronze sheet having a thickness of 2.0 to 2.3 mm, about $\frac{1}{8}$ digit. The main plate of the mechanism consists, however, of a pair of such plates placed together to form a double thickness. At one place, visible at the back of the main plate, near Axis M, where the back plate has broken away leaving the inner surface of the front plate visible there appears a raised (i.e., mirror image) letter H clearly visible with its serifs. This must mean that the inner surface of the front plate of this pair must have carried such an inscribed character. Like the letter T which is engraved inside the drum which may be either a crank handle or a Moon Dial, and perhaps also the letters H and Σ on the small subsidiary dials within the upper and lower back dials respectively,[13] I suppose the letter to have been a mark for correct location. Similar key letters are still used today in hand-assembled clockwork, and the tradition of key letters in geometrical and astronomical diagrams is attested from numerous Hellenistic examples. If this interpretation is correct it implies that the two plates could be taken apart and put together. I suggest, therefore, that there were originally two quite separate mechanism assemblies, one on the front plate and the other on the back. Each of these assemblies was probably self-contained, not requiring the support of the dial plate which seems also to have been removable. The two mechanism assemblies could then be put together back to back, and the wheels and axes that ran through both plates could then be fixed together by wedge and slot devices and squared axles.

Reviewing the sequence of plates and components in their arrangement through the thickness of the complete mechanism we have the following:

a) front door plate(s)
b) front dial plate and parapegma plates

---

[12] See A. G. Drachmann, *The Crank in Graeco-Roman Antiquity*, in Mikulas Teich and Robert Young (eds.), *Changing Perspectives in the History of Science* (London, Heinemann, 1973), pp. 33–51.

[13] It is also possible that these stand for H[ΛΙΟΣ] (Sun and Σ[ΕΛΗΝΗ] (Moon) respectively.

c) Sun and Moon indicator plates, perhaps also a block of planetary gearing if this is to be conjecturally restored
d) contrate Wheel *A* and input axle
e) Main Drive Wheel assembly on Axis *B*
f) front main plate
g) back main plate
h) differential turntable assembly on Axis *E*
i) back dial plate
j) back door plate(s)

From the thickness of Fragment B and from the remains of the lower back dial on the back of Fragment A it is easy to measure that the back dial plate must have been separated from the back main plate by a distance of about 13 mm, sufficient for about six layers of gearing. I suggest that together with the plate thickness this would correspond with almost one digit of a Roman foot, which may well have been the intention.

For the thickness of the front assembly, it must be noted that the well-preserved contrate Gear *A* of diameter 27.8 mm rises in place so that its axis is about 22 mm above the level of the front main plate and its top about 36 mm above the same level. The minimum possible total thickness for this assembly is therefore *ca.* 40 mm, but I feel it is more likely that the contrate gear would be placed either just halfway through the thickness of this assembly or halfway through the combined thickness of the front and back assemblies. In the first case the thickness of the front assembly would be 48 mm or about 3 digits, and in the second case it would be 65 mm or about $3\frac{1}{2}$ digits. The first arrangement, with the input to the mechanism being symmetrically placed within the front assembly gives therefore a combined thickness for the two sections together of just 4 digits or a quarter of a Roman foot. This would make the casing designed on a box of just one, by one-half, by one-quarter foot, and the neatness and regularity of this makes it somewhat preferable to the other choices admissible from the incomplete evidence available.

From the three reasonably well-preserved straight edges of the main plate it appears that it was not quite so wide as either the front or the back dial plates. It was also much shorter than the back dial plate but longer than that of the front dial. Since it appears that all the dial axles passed freely through the dial plates without needing them for support, the plates must have been retained at their appropriate distances from the main plate by spacers. The remains on both the front and back of the main plate indicate that wooden spacers were used, running in channels fixed along the edge in the front and just inside the edge at the back of the main plate. In addition to these side supports there may have been cross pieces. It is not quite certain, but I fancy I see traces of such a cross piece at the lower left edge of the front of Fragment A in the radiographs, and also in the older photographs there appears to be a thick edge for some distance which would give a complete corner of wooden support and channel structure in that region. Such a support would have been needed if the parapegma plates were fixed above and below the front dial so that I have assumed their existence in the reconstruction of the casing.

THE DOOR PLATES AND THE GENERAL ORIENTATION AND USE OF THE MECHANISM

It has already been remarked that a great deal has been preserved of a back door plate, inscribed on its inner face which fitted directly over the back dial plate and seems to have contained a text describing the cycles on which the mechanism is based. Portions of this text are preserved, in mirror image traces on Fragment B.1, and on both mirror image and a piece of the direct inscription on Fragment A.2, the back of the main plate. In all cases the inscription reads from top to bottom down the main length of the mechanism. The inscription on the back dial plate also reads in this same direction, so it is quite clear that, from the back at least, the mechanism is to be viewed in this direction only. One cannot quite tell from the length of lines on the inscription whether it is in a single column or in two. If in two we might well have had a pair of double doors opening like a triptych rather than a single door hinged on one side. I suspect that the more elegant and well-balanced style of double doors was used and in this case the preserved fragments of inscription may constitute the greater part of the line width.

One cannot be quite certain, but there are indications that a similar arrangement was used on the front of the instrument. The jumbled condition of the elements preserved make the original alignment difficult to see, and there are some doubts about the orientation of the zodiac circle and the parapegma, but the most appropriate layout would also seem to be that the front dial also was designed to be read from top to bottom in the same direction with a pair of columns of text and parapegma calendar both above and below the dial. The orientation of the zodiac circle would match better the style used on later astrolabes, if one supposed, however, that the dial was to be viewed with the left-hand edge as top and the right-hand edge as bottom; in that case the parapegma would have to be placed on strips each one column wide to the left and the right of the dial. Such an arrangement is just possible, but in that case I would see no good reason for the piece of the strip that is preserved to have a terminal edge between Σ and T.

Not much help in deciding the orientation of the front system is obtainable from the plate that seems to have been a door covering the dial plate in the same way as on the back. This fragment inscribed in the

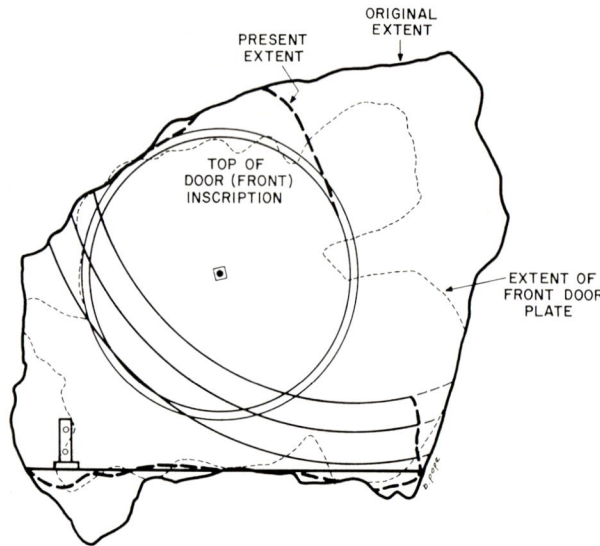

Fig. 10. Fragment C.1 with front door plate fragment.

small letter style, readily distinguishable from the medium letters of the back door and dial plate, and the large letters of the parapegma inscription is not to be found among the fragments published by Svoronos. It is preserved as a detached plate made of many small pieces of plate joined together, apparently in the original cleaning and restoration, and is of irregular outline and outside dimensions approximately 144 mm in width and 95 mm top to bottom. I strongly suspect that originally this was accreted over the parapegma plate on the Fragment C.1 of Svoronos and it was for this reason that this important and clear inscription was not read or published in the earliest work on the Antikythera wreck. If indeed this is so it would have been in just the right position, covering the front dial plate with its divided month and zodiac circles. It is of more or less the correct dimensions to correspond with the large diminution in size of Fragment C which is apparent on comparing the early with the modern photographs of this piece. One cannot be quite sure of the original orientation, but I feel it is a better fit with the photographs if one aligns the preserved fragment with its text on the outside face and reading from top to bottom in the same sense as that used in the back of the instrument and as that given by the preferred orientation of the parapegma columns in the front, i.e., above and below the main dial rather than at the sides. Here again one cannot tell whether a single door or a pair was used, but it seems large enough to cover more than half the width unless the door plate has been displaced by distortion.

The entire instrument must then be viewed in the same vertical position. It could either be placed flat down on a table and seen one side at a time, or mounted vertically so that the front doors and the back door(s) could be opened at the same time. I feel the latter alternative is more elegant and likely but one cannot quite exclude the possibility that the whole instrument was portable and capable of being placed on a table and turned over at will. The door plates are quite thin and would have been very flimsy protection for the rather fragile dial and pointer systems but the plates may have been mounted on wooden panels that would have been easier to hinge than metal plates and that would have given more protection. If the instrument were portable and used in this flat position we would almost certainly have to say that the entire mechanism was designed to be adjusted by a handle and it would then clearly be interpreted as functioning as a demonstration calculator for the calendric cycles built into the dials and gearwork.

If, on the other hand, as seems a little more likely, the entire box were mounted on a pedestal of some sort in an upright position the front and back doors could be opened together and all dials would be visible in a more impressive way. Also in that case, although the device might still have a handle and function in the way described above, it could alternatively be driven automatically by connecting the shaft from the contrate wheel to a waterclock, perhaps through a worm drive moving tooth by tooth on a daily basis. Perhaps even the shaft coming out of the side of the casing could be concealed in the supports for the instrument. It seems a likely possibility in keeping with the style of the period that the device could be mounted on the arms of an appropriate statue, perhaps on Urania, or a pair of Urania and Atlas. The drive shaft might be concealed in an arm or by drapery and connected to the clepsydra and anaphoric clock and perhaps also a jackwork display to go with it.

In this latter case the Antikythera mechanism would function not as a calculator but as a portion of one of the traditional exhibition pieces designed to be set up in a temple or in a structure like the Tower of Winds; it would be completely in line with the later history of complicated astronomical clockwork. There is perhaps a remote possibility that one of the statues from the Antikythera wreck should be a support for the instrument, but I can suggest no likely candidate from those preserved and published.

It perhaps is worth remarking that, even if one interprets the evidence so as to reconstruct the Antikythera mechanism as a portable hand calculator for calendrical cycles, it can have absolutely nothing to do with navigation. It is certainly not part of the ship's instruments as has often been supposed, but a valuable art object taken with the rest of the load.

THE ACCURACY OF ESTIMATING GEAR TEETH NUMBERS

In no place in the extant fragments of the Antikythera mechanism is even a single gear wheel preserved in such an uncorroded state that all of its teeth could be counted visually or in the radiographs. If it were, one could unequivocally state the number of gear teeth and there would be no room for error. Since it is not, there must be various strategems to estimate the number with various degrees of probable error. A great deal of the astronomical interpretation hangs upon the attendant uncertainty.

Where a reasonably long stretch of gear teeth can be seen and counted by the naked eye or on the radiographs it is possible to extrapolate to the entire circle. Even in this case there are two sources of potential error. One cannot be sure that the original gear was divided perfectly evenly, and one cannot be sure in some cases of exact location of the center and therefore of the size of the circle to which one is extrapolating.

UNEVEN DIVISION

The gear may have been divided in an uneven manner either by accident or by design. We know from the detailed measurement of the preserved parts of divided circle from the front dial (see p. 19) that, even when accurate division was clearly intended, the graduations fall into their theoretical places only to an average accuracy of plus or minus a quarter of a degree, and to an error which rises to a maximum displacement of almost half a degree over a 30° segment of arc. For even the largest gear wheel in the Antikythera mechanism this source of error could not alter the tooth

Fig. 12. Front of Fragment A, present state. A.1.

count by as much as a single unit, since in a wheel of 240 teeth each tooth subtends 1°30′ and the maximum error corresponds to one-third of tooth.

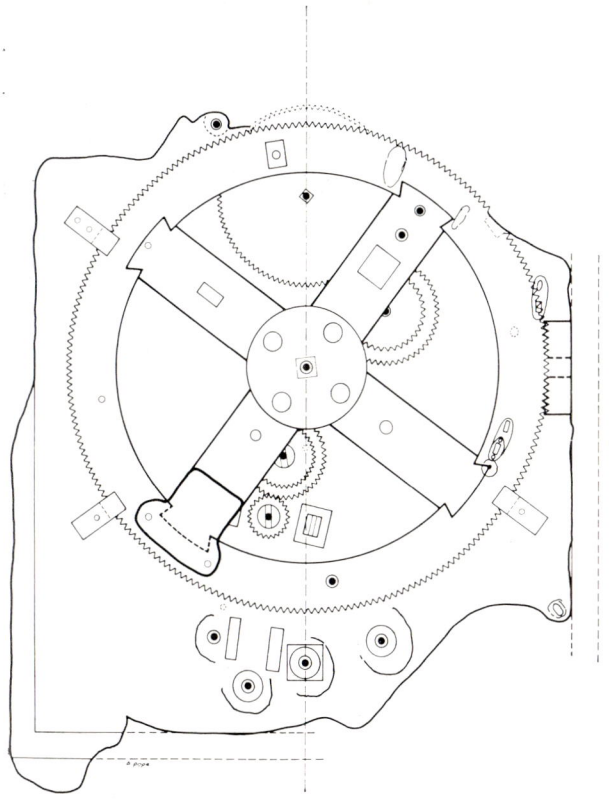

Fig. 11. Schematic of front of main fragment.

Fig. 13. Front of Fragment A, before cleaning. A.1.

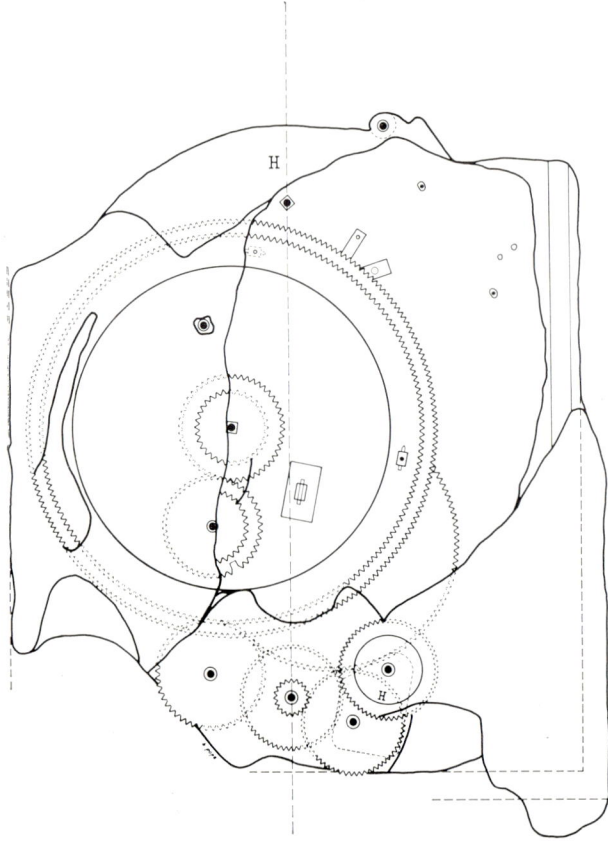

FIG. 14. Schematic of back of main fragment.

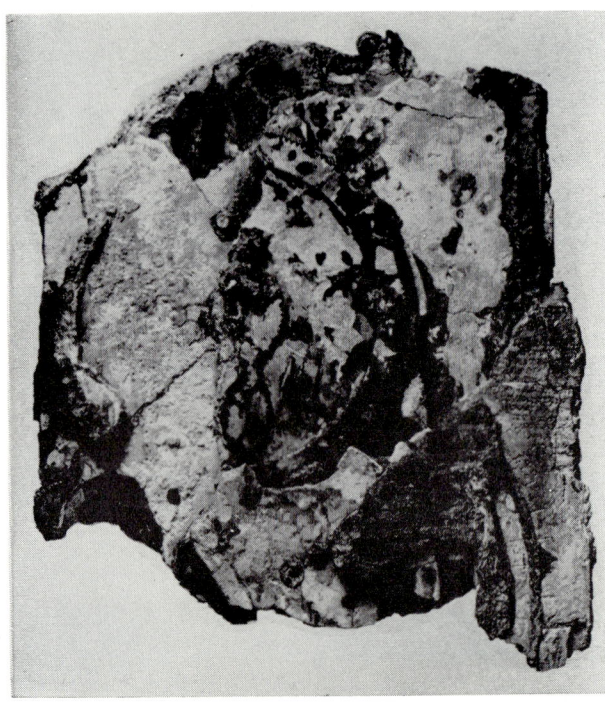

FIG. 15. Back of Fragment A, present state. A.2.

FIG. 16. Back of Fragment A, before cleaning. A.2.

Uneven division produced by design may be much more misleading. In various Renaissance and modern pieces of geared clockwork, particularly in planetary models, I have seen the rather slipshod technique of producing, for example, a gear of 31 teeth by first marking out a gear of 32 and then slightly widening the teeth in a single quadrant of it to contain only seven instead of eight. If one attempted to reconstruct such a gear from any part of its normal three quadrants the count deduced would be 32, and if the altered quadrant only were preserved, the inference would be that the complete gear must have had 28 teeth. It is possible that such a technique may have been used to produce the suggested count of 127 teeth for gear $D2$ and the 38 teeth for gear $C1$, and if so these wheels would probably be of sizes appropriate to wheels of 128 and 36 teeth respectively.

ERROR IN LOCATION OF CENTER

In most cases the axles on which the gear wheels were mounted are of diameter 2–4 mm, and corrosion often makes it difficult to see the entire circle and locate its center with complete accuracy. I estimate that an error of 0.5 mm is entirely plausible in most cases, and this, given the normal tooth size, will correspond to an error of two teeth in the total count. This error will occur equally whether the location of the center is used for visual measurement of the radius of the wheel or for the radiographic technique of constructing the circle of best fit for the extant teeth. In most of the cases where my best estimate of a tooth

Fig. 17a. Fragment B.1., present state.

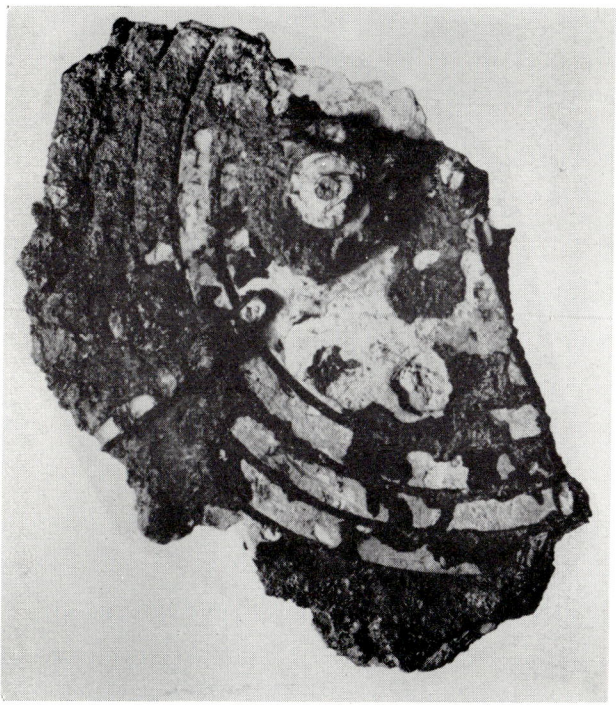

Fig. 17c. Fragment B.2., present state.

count has differed from that of Karakalos an effect of this nature and magnitude seems to have been involved.

In addition to these types of error there is a special and insidious difficulty in measuring corroded fragments of gearing and attempting to derive from this the geometry of the gear trains.

Fig. 17b. Fragment B.1., before cleaning.

ERROR IN DETERMINING RADIUS

In all the places where teeth are well preserved we find that their shape is almost exactly that of an equilateral triangle, except for the main drive wheel, Gear $B1$, where the teeth are rather larger than normal and also slightly longer in relation to their width so that the tooth angle must be a little less than 60°. If two such wheels are meshed together they will not, of course, run quite so smoothly as those of modern epicycloidal design, but nevertheless there will exist an effective radius which comes about halfway along the length of a tooth and which will mark the boundary between the two wheels and thereby give the gear ratio. It follows that if one is attempting, as here, to relate tooth counts and radii for such wheels, the radius must be measured up to a point about halfway along the total length of the teeth. For equilateral teeth the radial length of each tooth is $\sqrt{3}/2$ times the distance between two adjacent teeth. If by mistake or because of obscurity caused by corrosion the radius of the wheel is taken to the outer or the inner edge of the teeth instead of the center it will cause an error of $2\pi \cdot \sqrt{3}/4 = 2.7$ teeth above or below the proper tooth count. Errors of this sort, particularly those of overestimation must be rather frequent, so I suppose that there is always a possibility that the count derived from the radius measurement may run up to two or three teeth too high. Where errors larger than this occur I suppose they are due to other considerations such as the use, in some places, notable on the large gears of the main drive

Fig. 18a. Fragment C.1., present state.

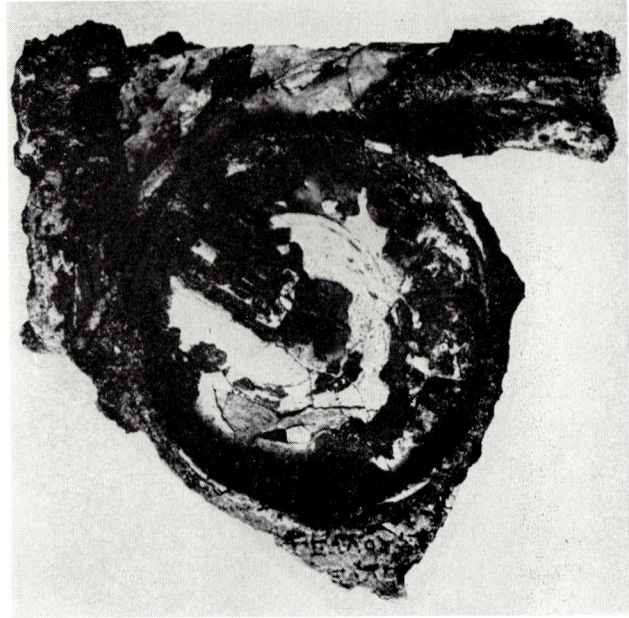

Fig. 19a. Fragment C.2., present state.

Fig. 18b. Fragment C.1., after partial cleaning.

Fig. 18c. Fragment C.1., before cleaning.

Fig. 19b. Fragment C.2., before cleaning.

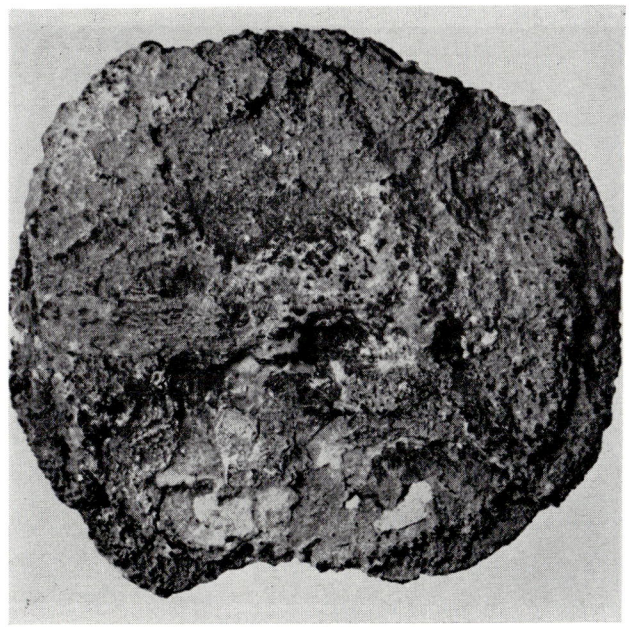

FIG. 20a. Fragment D outside, present state.

FIG. 20b. Fragment D inside, present state.

wheel and of the differential turntable, of a tooth size different from that of the rest of the gearing of the mechanism.

DESCRIPTION OF INDIVIDUAL GEARS

GEAR A

This is a massive crown or contrate wheel, preserved in its original position, engaging with the main drive wheel $B1$ and in a plane at right angles to it. The body of the wheel consists of a cylindrical block of radius 13.9 mm and thickness 7.0 mm, but the teeth project out an additional 2.1 mm beyond the inner face of the block. Because of the position of the block and the fact that very few teeth are preserved and visible, it is very difficult to get a tooth count from direct measurement or the radiographs. The tooth size seems to correspond, as one would expect, with that of the drive wheel, rather greater than that of the rest of the gearing of the mechanism, i.e., about 1.75 mm between teeth rather than 1.57 mm. At this spacing the crown gear would have about 50 teeth, and if one supposes that the number is determined also by ease of division the nearest round values would be 45 or 48. Probably the crown wheel makes exactly or approximately 5 revolutions for every one of the main drive wheel; the ratio seems without astronomical significance except perhaps that 5 is a factor of 365 so that the handle would turn (and possibly also be graduated) in exactly 73 days. More probably, the function is simply to transmit motion from a handle without further calibration or indication.

The construction of this wheel is hard to see but fine cracks suggest that it was made from a cylindrical block with a strip soldered round it to form a band in which the gear teeth could be cut. The axis of the cylinder is pierced completely by a rectangular hole, 5.6 mm by 7.4 mm so that an axle could be fitted without turning; such an axle would necessarily have a diameter greater than 9.3 mm and at its other end would be fitted the folding crank handle preserved at the back of the remaining fragment of the front dial. The drum of this handle has at its center an appropriate squared hole for such a shaft.

This crown wheel is preserved in place by surrounding debris from the side wall of the mechanism casing, possibly originally of wood but now heavily accreted with calcified deposits. Above and below the wheel, displaced somewhat to the left there remain also two supporting pillars and lugs which now adhere to and rise from the top of the drive wheel. These pillars rise to heights of about 21 mm and 24 mm above the top level of the drive wheel, and are, therefore, some 30 mm above the level of the main plate. It seems highly probable that these pillars originally flanked the crown wheel and acted as spacers to keep it in its place between the main plate and a top dial plate.

GEAR $B1$

This main drive wheel, preserved almost intact, is perhaps the most obvious feature of the extant fragments. It consists of an annular rim connected to a circular hub by four wide spokes. The rim of outer radius 63.0 mm (Svoronos says 65.5 mm) and inner radius 52.5 mm has around the limb a well preserved stretch of teeth, rather larger than those of the rest of the mechanism. In an arc of 60° I count slightly more than 38 teeth which would yield a total count of 228+, but from the radiographs Karakalos finds a lower limit of 223 and an upper limit of 226. There seems no evidence that this main drive wheel meshes with any gearing other than the crown wheel which turns it and thence the entire mechanism, so one may suppose that the number of teeth is dictated only by convenience. We take, therefore, within the range offered the sole round value, 225 teeth, which gives a 5/1 ratio with the crown wheel at 45 teeth. At this count the distance between teeth is 1.75 mm.

The spokes in the one o'clock and seven o'clock positions are each 15.6 mm wide and those in the four o'clock and ten o'clock positions are 17.3 mm wide. The four spokes are mortised into the rim, soldered in place, and fixed also by a rivet. The hub is a circular plate 18.2 mm in radius, slightly larger than the gear $B2$ which it covers. The four spokes are fixed under the hub by one large rivet each, and at the center of the hub is visible a 6.3 mm square hole, with its diagonals aligned in the spoke directions, for a non-slip axle and at its center a smaller circular depression for the inner shaft on this axis. The join between the rim and the spoke at the seven o'clock positions seems to have been broken and then repaired by a thin T-shaped plate which covers the outer portion of the spoke and has been fixed to the rim with rivets and presumably also soldering.

This main drive wheel preserves clear evidence of some sort of superstructure mounted over it. The spoke in the ten o'clock position has a lug mounted on it 8.3 mm long, 3.9 mm wide and standing 6.3 mm above the surface of the wheel. The three other spokes contain holes indicating that they may also have had similar lugs on them and in addition there is a square depression on the spoke in the one o'clock position. Furthermore, on the rim, exactly midway between each of the spoke positions, there are traces of former fixtures. In the eleven o'clock position is a rectangular depression with a rivet hole at the center; in the eight o'clock position just the rivet hole remains, and the other two corresponding places are obscured by debris. The evidence seems to suggest that pillars rising from these four places on the rim and another four on the spokes supported some sort of plate above and parallel with that of the drive wheel, turning with it. The pair of axles available for turning indicators for the Sun and the Moon are so geared that they go in opposite directions around the zodiac. This cannot be so, and one of them must be reversed. The most simple assumption is to suppose the inner axle gives correctly the lunar rotation and that instead of reversing the direction of the outer axle a second wheel engaging with the contrate Wheel A is used for the solar indicator. Since there is therefore an indication that there was another similar wheel above, turned by the other side of the crown wheel and serving as a central dial plate for the main front dial, indicating the solar position, this spacing may have been part of a system keeping the two oppositely turning large wheels apart.

Alternatively there is a possibility that this space between the large wheels may have held a gearing system, now totally vanished, which served to exhibit the rotations of all of the planets other than the Sun and Moon. If such gearing was to be part of the device it would be most appropriate at this place where annual and monthly rotations were available just under the front dial plate.

The main drive wheel is held so that its top surface is about 6.4 mm above the level of the main plate. It has to leave clear space between the wheel and the main plate equivalent to the thickness of the two gears on axis C and the two on axis L. To keep the large wheel from bending or tilting on its axis there are supporting spacers around the rim, two being preserved on the left side, 60° above and below the line joining axes A and B, and on the right side only the lower one remains. The spacers, shaped like an h, seem to have been cut from blocks, are slotted so that the drive wheel can just run freely, and have their long sides rivetted to the main plate. In addition to these spacers the radiographs show the presence of parts of a ring-shaped strip lying below the rim of this plate and keeping it an even distance above the main plate.

GEAR $B2$

This gear of radius 16.4 mm is slightly smaller than the hub plate of the main drive wheel and is visible directly beneath it. It must be separated from the main plate of the mechanism either by a washer one gear thick, or perhaps by the gear $B3$ if this lies above rather than below the main plate—the evidence is not conclusive since a section cannot be seen or revealed by the radiographs. At the standard gear tooth spacing wheel of this size should have about 65 teeth. Karakalos counts a lower limit of 64 and an upper of 66. I suggest from its meshing with the gears C–D and with L–M–N that the round number of 64 teeth gives the best fit.

GEARS $B3$ AND $B4$

These two gears cannot be seen by the naked eye and are visible only from the radiographs as a somewhat blurred double image just half the size of $B2$. Karakalos counts 32 teeth, and this is the most reasonable number to assume for the gear trains involved in both gears. The wheel $B4$ is certainly located between the base plate and the differential turntable, but it is uncertain whether $B3$ is above or below the main plate. It is perhaps most sensible to consider that $B3$ be above the plate for then it also serves as a spacer necessary to keep $B2$ separated from the base plate by the required thickness of an extra wheel. Thus although it cannot be seen in this position the assumption has been made in the plan reconstruction.

Fig. 21. Radiograph of Fragment A seen from front. The contrate gear A is on the right, the rings of the lower back dial are at the bottom left.

GEARS $C1$ AND $C2$

This pair of gears, rigidly fixed together, the smaller on top, are of radii 9.3 mm and 10.6 mm corresponding at the standard spacing to tooth counts of 37 and 42. The actual counts which I accept, made by Karakalos from the radiographs, are 38 and 48, showing that the larger wheel is cut with rather smaller teeth than usual. This is confirmed by the fact that the pinion $D1$ with which it engages has correspondingly small teeth. I feel this has been dictated by the fact that in this place alone one has two different gear systems joining a single pair of axes. The centers B and D are linked on the one hand by the gearing $B4$–$D2$, and on the other hand by the chain of gears $B2 - C1 + C2 - D1$. The first pair totals $32 + 127 = 159$ teeth,

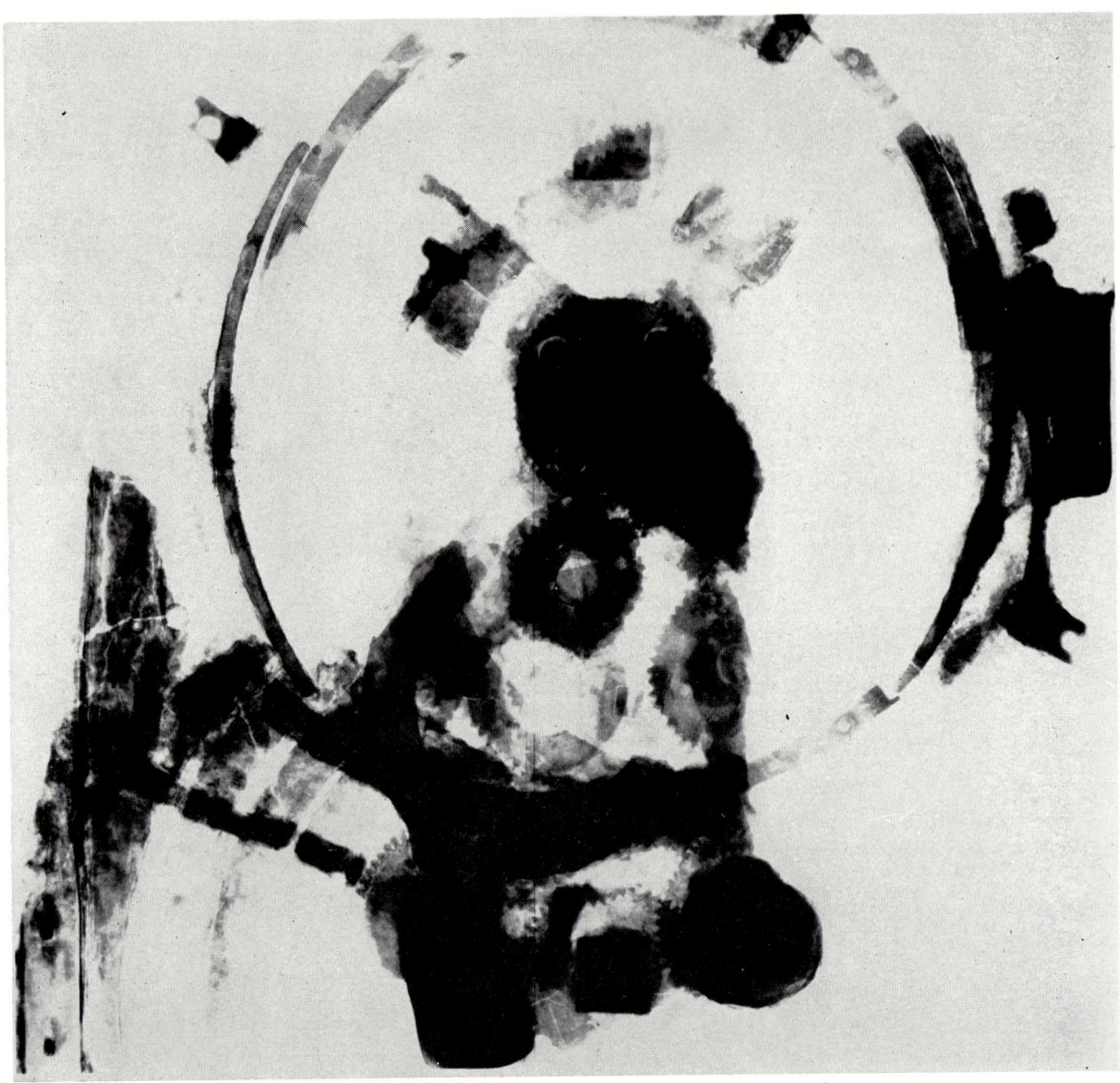

Fig. 22. The same with higher penetration showing inner gearing.

and of the chain the first pair comprises $64 + 38 = 102$ teeth leaving a gap of 57 teeth in which to establish a 2/1 ratio. This could be done exactly by a wheel pair of $38 - 19$, but those are awkward numbers and presumably the choice of having $48 - 24$ in smaller teeth has yielded easier gear cutting and a much more even pinion. The wheel pair is fixed in place by a wedge and pin running through the circular axle.

PINION $D1$

This small gear wheel has a radius of 5.4 mm corresponding to 22 teeth, but as above, one has a direct count of 24 teeth, necessarily rather smaller than usual. It is fixed in place by a wedge and pin running through a circular axle, but since it must turn the wheel $D2$ on the other side of the plate there must be a squared end on the axle and at the center of the pinion. The pinion is fixed in place and retained against becoming disengaged by a small displacement by means of a bridge which has been erected on a pair of rectangular supports which flank the small wheel. The top of the bridge is now lacking and only the supports with their wedge and slot fittings remain. The bridge must have had a width of 11.8 mm, just a shade larger than the 10.9 mm diameter of the pinion, and its length to the outsides of the rectangular supports is 32.5 mm. The line of the axis BD runs about 14° to the left of the central axis of the mechanism, but there is some slight indication that BCD are not collinear, but that the center C may be displaced slightly to the right. The displacement is, however, at the most 1 mm and this may be due to distortion during the corrosion of the fragments.

Fig. 23. Sample of alignment radiographs showing teeth, wheel circles, axes, etc., marked in ink for tracing the gear trains.

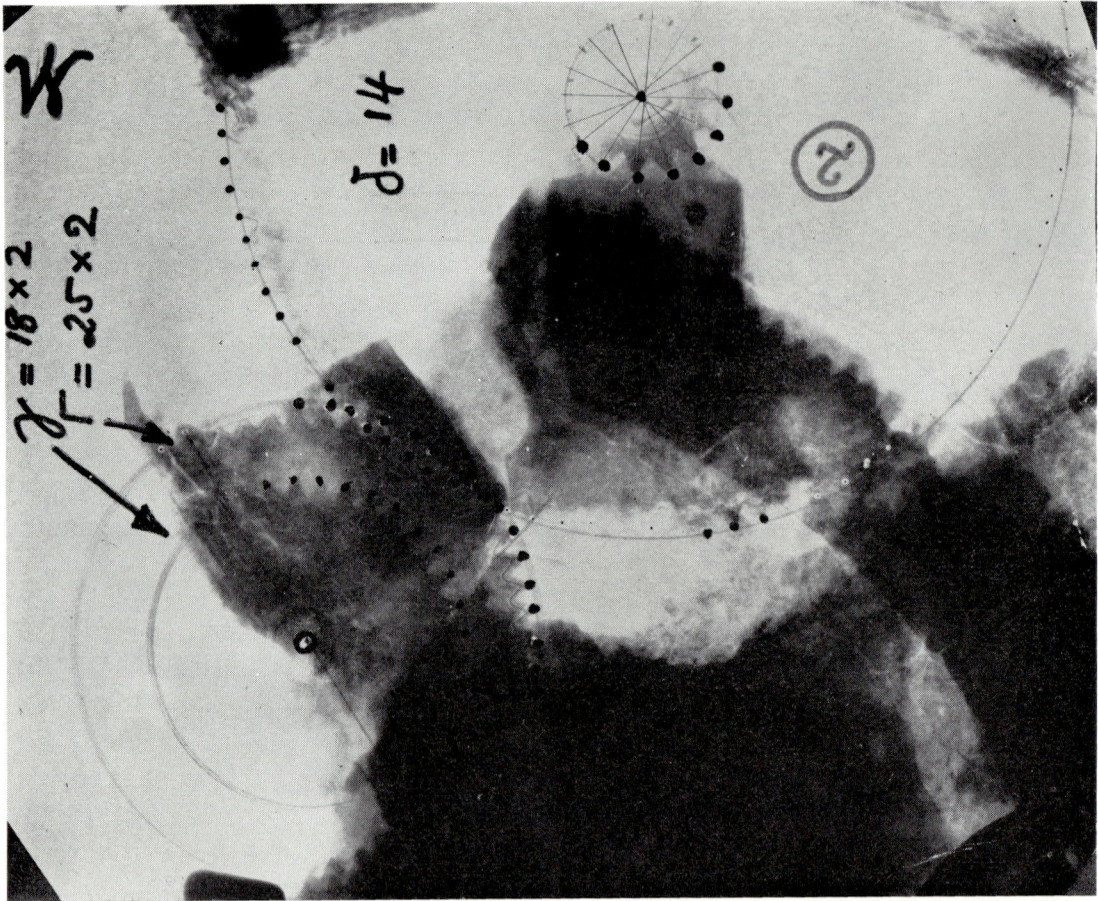

Fig. 24. Sample of tooth-count radiograph enlargements showing method used to determine meshing in gear trains.

GEAR D2

The center of this gear is hidden under the differential turntable and only a small portion of the geared edge is visible to the naked eye. I estimate from the visible portion a radius of ca. 33 mm corresponding to a gear count of ca. 132, but Karakalos, from the radiographs showing a much larger extent, counts 128. From the gear train I suggest that the actual number should be 127 which is the vital parameter needed to produce 254 siderial revolutions of the Moon in 19 solar years (it is the gear C1 of 38 teeth which provides the essential parameter for the number of years). Presumably this wheel, too, must be mounted on a squared axle so as to turn rigidly with D1.

GEARS E1 AND E2

These, like B3 and B4, are visible only as a blurred multiple outline on radiographs taken through the many layers of material at this point. They appear similar in size to that previous pair and Karakalos agrees tentatively with counts of 32 teeth for these too. A small extant fragment visible on the back plate near the break line through the differential turntable suggests a radius of a little less than 9 mm which is consistent with this count. Wheel E1 is probably on the front of the main plate and happens to be in such a position that quite by chance it is completely covered by that drive wheel spoke in the four o'clock position. Gear E1 meshes with B3 and serves to transmit the annual revolutions of the main drive wheel without change of speed to gear E5 on the top of the turntable. Gear E2 is an idler on the main turntable shaft which transmits the siderial revolutions of the Moon to the underside of the turntable. It is necessarily a double wheel of two equal portions rigidly fixed together, since E2ii with J and K1 must lie in a plane above that of E2i and B4/D2 so that the turntable can revolve on its axis E, carrying J and K1 with it. A single idler wheel could not affect this and free rotation could not occur. I am most grateful to Prof. A. W. Sleeswyk of Groningen for pointing out to me this matter on which I had been in error in a previous reconstruction.

GEARS E3 AND E4

The larger of these gears, E4, is a disc 52.4 mm in radius (Svoronos gives 52.0 mm and Theophanides gives 52.5 mm) which constitutes the main plate of the differential turntable. The smaller gear, E3, consists of

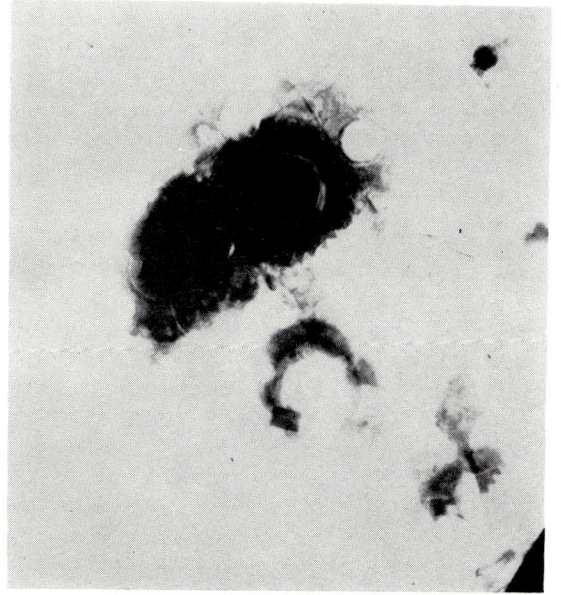

FIG. 25. Sample of detail radiograph. In this case attention is focussed at the center of axis B to see the structure at the center and count teeth for wheels B3., B4., E1., E2.

FIG. 27. Radiograph of Fragment C.

FIG. 26. Radiograph of Fragment B.

an annulus of outside radius 50.2 mm (Theophanides 50.5 mm) and inside radius 41.8 mm. The annulus is fixed above the turntable by means of at least two, more probably four wedge and pin fittings evenly spaced around it; only one of these can now be seen. The sizes of the gears would indicate tooth counts of 201 and 210 respectively, but Karakalos counts from the much more extensive radiographic evidence 192 and 222 which would imply that one wheel has smaller and the other larger teeth than normal. The count for $E3$ makes it yield an exact and simple ratio, $192/48 = 4/1$, which is in good agreement with the astronomical parameters since it provides an axis G which will turn once per synodic month and move a pointer over the main lower back dial at this useful rate. Unfortunately the larger gear, $E4$, engages with no other preserved wheel. It is possible that it could be connected by gearing, now totally lacking, to one of the subsidiary small dials on the upper back dial, the central dial of which has a pointer revolving in a four-year cycle. If so, the number of teeth strongly urges some connection with the 223-month eclipse cycle attested by the one coherent piece of epigraphic evidence where this number of months is inscribed together with the 235-month cycle.

The evidence of the radiographs and the naked eye suggests that the turntable was supported and held in place in a similar way to the main drive wheel. On the top right-hand corner there are partial remains of a spacer support, and the radiographs show strips of a spacer underlying the turntable and separating it from the main base plate at several points. Both $E3$ and $E4$ are of thickness 1.6 mm and the bottom of the turntable is raised to a height of 2.7 mm above the main base plate, the intervening space therefore has room for just two minimally thin gears in between.

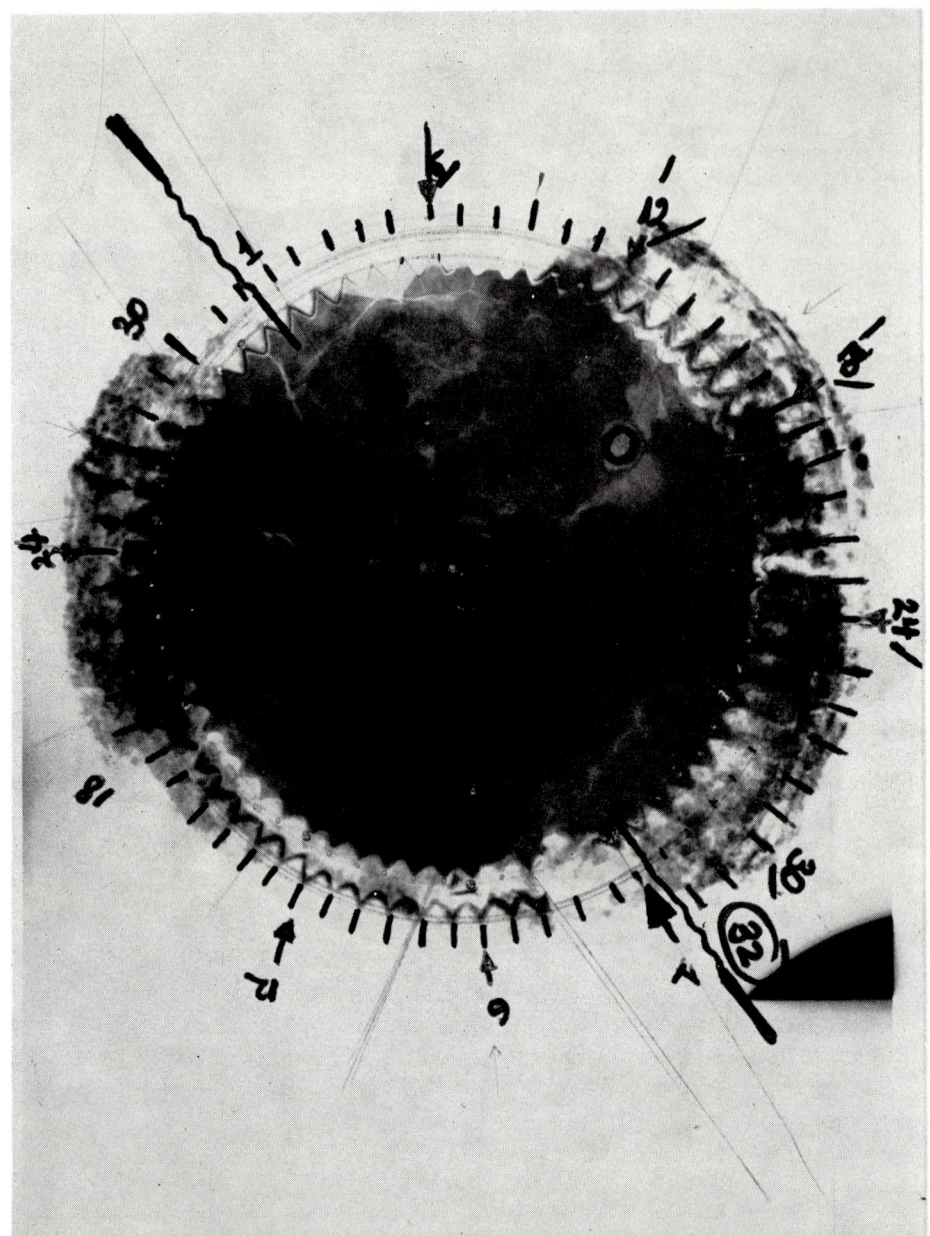

Fig. 28. Radiograph of Fragment D. This photograph, the only one in which a gear wheel is almost complete, has been used for the tooth-count process.

GEAR E5

This gear is clearly visible lying above the center of the differential turntable, forming a pair with the equal sized gear K2 mounted next to it, eccentrically on the turntable. I measure the radii of these two gears as 13.7 and 14.6 mm respectively, but the distance between their centers is only 27.2 mm so presumably there has been some slight distortion enlarging K2. The average size of the wheels corresponds to a tooth count of about 54 teeth for each, but Karakalos counts 50–52 teeth for E5 and 51 and 48 for K2 which he sees as a double wheel. I feel that the apparent double thickness of both of these gears is caused by much corroded spacing washers underneath them. Further, since the apparent purpose is simply to provide a 1/1 gear ratio I feel that some round number is most likely for the count of each and suggest the lowest of the observed numbers, 48 teeth, as being appropriate. The sum of the two gear counts, 96 teeth, can also then be neatly matched on the back of the turntable by two pairs, each of 32 teeth meshing with a missing idler wheel of 64 teeth, and forming a neat equilateral triangle. At the center of E5 is a squared axle hole aligned with the line EK, that however must be accidental since E5 turns rigidly fixed to $K2$ but not to the body of the turntable. What seems to be a retaining plate holding the tops of $E5$ and $K2$ together lies between the two wheels and is preserved over the latter wheel as a cap of radius *ca.* 9 mm.

GEARS $F1$ AND $F2$

Only part of the edge of $F1$ is visible to the naked eye, but the pair, fixed rigidly together and mounted on a small circular block is quite plain in the radiographs. The larger wheel, $F1$, is mounted next to the block and is supported at the same level as $E3$ with which it meshes. On the radiograph it would seem to come very close to meshing also with $D2$, but that latter wheel is mounted directly on the main base plate far below the level of $F1$. The smaller wheel $F2$ is mounted directly above $F1$. Karakalos counts the wheel pair as 54 and 30 teeth respectively, but I view the former number as an overestimate in view of the fact that a simple ratio with the 192 teeth of $E3$ seems to be intended. I have settled on assessing the meshing pair as $48/192 = 4/1$, but $54/216$ would give the same ratio and perhaps fit the observed count for the smaller wheel and the diameter for the larger one at least as well.

GEARS $G1$ AND $G2$

Again, as with F we have a pair of wheels fixed rigidly together and mounted on a block at the appropriate height above the main base plate. The rather thick square block in this case is slightly larger than the smaller gear, $G1$, and it raises the larger gear, $G2$, to be on the same level as $F2$ with which it meshes. Again the smaller gear is above the larger, nearer to the dial plate above through which the axle extends with a circular (unsquared) end. Karakalos counts 20 teeth for the small gear, which I accept, but 54 or 55 teeth for the larger of the pair. I find this too small for any simple and meaningful interpretation of the gear train and suggest that the count here should be 60 teeth, giving a gear ratio of $60/30 = 2/1$.

GEARS $H1$ AND $H2$

Once more the wheel pair is mounted on a block, even higher than the previous one so that the lower, larger of the pair is at the same height as the smaller of the previous pair. Thus $H2$ is mounted on the level of $G1$. The block used is much larger than the previous ones, a single block serving to carry both this pair and the next in the train, I. The block is cut away and slotted to allow free passage of $G2$ and cut at the back to give room for $D2$. For this pair Karakalos counts 60 to 62 for the larger and 16 teeth for the smaller. I have no trouble in accepting the count of 60, since $60/20 = 3/1$, but suggest that the 16 should be corrected to 15 so as to make a simple ratio with the wheel of 60 with which it meshes. An alternative to the latter would, of course, be $16/64$ but Karakalos counts I as 60 teeth which I find acceptable, the context being a train of gears producing a $1/12$ ratio by using three gears of 60 teeth each together with two pinions giving reductions of $1/3$ and $1/4$.

GEAR I

This wheel is completely invisible except for a small fragment near the lower edge; Karakalos counts it at 60 teeth from the radiographs, see above. On the dial plate above this gear is inscribed an ungraduated circle inscribed with a letter H (Greek *eta*) which constitutes a subsidiary dial inside the lower back dial.

GEAR J

Nothing of this gear wheel is extant. It is restored conjecturally partly on the basis of a mechanical necessity to connect the otherwise disconnected wheels $E2$ and $K1$, and it must be remembered that the first of these is also conjectural to some degree since it is visible only on the radiographs and may be a ghost of the wheel $E1$ of exactly the same size and position in plan. It is, however, also postulated that J exists on the basis of the axle fitting which is plainly visible as an otherwise inexplicable peg and wedge construction placed so as to form an exact equilateral triangle with the axes E and K. As remarked above (*sub* Gear $E5$) an idler wheel of 64 teeth at this point, meshing with the two 32-toothed wheels on the underside of the turntable would explain and utilize this equilateral triangle construction and let the turntable operate as a differential gear system subtracting the siderial motion of the Sun from that of the Moon and causing the entire turntable to rotate at an angular velocity of one turn in two synodic months.

GEARS $K1$ AND $K2$

See above *sub* Gear $E5$. A most interesting feature occurs a little to the right of the lowest point of gear $K2$ where a small square slot is visible at the outer edge interrupting the row of gear teeth. I felt at first that this might have been some sort of "click" mechanism by which the revolution of this wheel might be counted as in the hodometers of Heron of Alexandria. The most probable explanation is that, however, which was advanced to me by the late L. C. Eichner when he was building a partial reconstruction of the mechanism for the Smithsonian Institution. Eichner points out that this feature is exactly what would remain if a tooth had been broken in antiquity by accident during construction or operation, and if the break had been repaired. The procedure for repair, then as now, would have been to cut such a slot, solder in a new strip of metal, and cut a new tooth on it. With the passage of time and the undersea corrosion the soldered metal join would have been eroded preferentially and have dropped out of place leaving the bare slot.

GEARS L1 AND L2

This is another pair of gear wheels rigidly fixed together, the smaller above the bigger. The fixed axle on which the pair rotates is visible on the back of the plate, appearing like a rivet head at the appropriate place where it has been revealed by the breaking away of the left-hand half of the turntable plate. The radii of this pair of gears are 8.7 mm and 13.0 mm corresponding to tooth counts of 35 and 52, but Karakalos finds 36+ and 52. From the trains I find 36 to be acceptable for the smaller but suggest the rounder number 54 for the larger. It might be remarked that BLM is a right angle and the sides that enclose it are of lengths corresponding as radii to tooth counts of exactly $64 + 36 = 100$ and $54 + 96 = 150$; this seems one of the few places where "drawing board geometry" seems to have determined the plan layout of the axes of the mechanism. It is perhaps also worth noting that the radius corresponding to 150 teeth, 37.5 mm is almost exactly two digits of which there were sixteen in the Roman foot of *ca.* 295.7 mm.[14]

GEARS M1 AND M2

The larger of these gears is a disc of 23.3 mm radius lying with its axis on the midline of the main base plate. It lies on the plate and meshes at that level with gear $L2$. The size would give 93 teeth but Karakalos counts 96+ over a well-preserved long stretch, and I find 96 quite acceptable. The gear has the usual squared hole, 2.7 mm square, at the center, the diagonal lying almost exactly, by accident, along the midline of the plate. Though hardly a trace remains visible there seems to be enough left of the Pinion $M2$ to be registered on the radiographs. Its size cannot be accurately determined, but Karakalos counts 14 teeth. In my opinion a slight re-estimation of the center leads one to 16 teeth as a much better fit and a more appropriate number for geometric division.

The radiographs show a puzzling feature, not visible to the naked eye, which lies near this pinion and is probably to be associated with it. Along the central axis of the main plate, just below the pinion, in a position where it is mostly obscured by Gears $E3$ and $E4$ and by corrosion products is a square plate fixed down by two rivets and appearing rather similar to those flanking the Pinion $D1$, except that I find no trace of a central pillar or wedge fitting to hold down a bridge. Furthermore, I am doubtful as to the existence of a similar plate placed symmetrically on the other side of the pinion above it on the center line. I had at first thought I saw traces on the radiographs but these may be accidental shadings, and if there were such an upper plate it would either have to be below the plate where it could not give much support or it would intervene between Gear N and the Pinion $M2$, preventing them from being on the same level and meshing. Perhaps the observed square plate is the base for some sort of one-sided support bracket which came over the top of the pinion, the greater part of which is now missing.

GEAR N

This is a detached fragment of mechanism (Svoronos, fragment D) which was seen by Rehm, but then misplaced in the museum and not refound until March, 1973. It is a highly calcified mass about 40 mm in diameter and 5 to 8.5 mm thick which appears in the radiographs to contain a single gear wheel which Karakalos counts at 63 teeth. Just possibly the great thickness and the blur which gives a double row of teeth might indicate that we are dealing here with a pair of identical or nearly similar wheels. The center shows a round hole with a wedge and pin fixing as in the axes of C and D. There are also three fixing (?) rivets or axes arranged in an equilateral triangle on the gear face. The fragment has a light band that matches the coloration and seems to fit at the center of the dial system, i.e., at the point a of Fragment B side 2 in Svoronos and therefore along the center line at the very top of the extant main fragment. An alternative place for a wheel of this size would be at the side of the lacking idler wheel, J, beneath the plate of the differential turntable, but in that case one would have to suppose that the wheel had already been displaced from its position and became calcified in isolation from the rest of the fragments. I feel there is just enough evidence of a physical fit to prefer the placement at axis N.

GEARS O1 AND O2

The remains of this gearing is a prominent feature of Svoronos's fragment B, side 2, point b. Because of much corrosion and calcification and also because of the great thickness and radio-opacity of the specimen it is most difficult to distinguish and measure details. There appears to be a single axis, probably unsquared, about 4 mm in diameter and extending to a depth of 12.5 mm behind the back level of this portion of dial plate. The first 5.4 mm of this depth appears to be filled with undifferentiated debris, but behind this is a gear wheel about 2.6 mm thick and about 13.5 to 14.0 mm in radius. This should correspond to about 54 teeth, but my best counts from visible and radiographic data give a consistently lower number, nearer to 48 teeth which I take provisionally to be the value. Behind this wheel is another smaller wheel also about 2.6 mm thick and 12.9 mm in diameter, but on this I find no visible teeth. The radiographs show rather indistinctly the presence of a smaller wheel, about 2/3 the size of the larger, hence very approximately 32 teeth, but I cannot place it and suppose it may be concealed in corrosion products within the 12.9 mm diameter mass.

---

[14] For this note on the Roman digit, in common use in all the Hellenistic area at this time, I am indebted to Miss Mabel Lang.

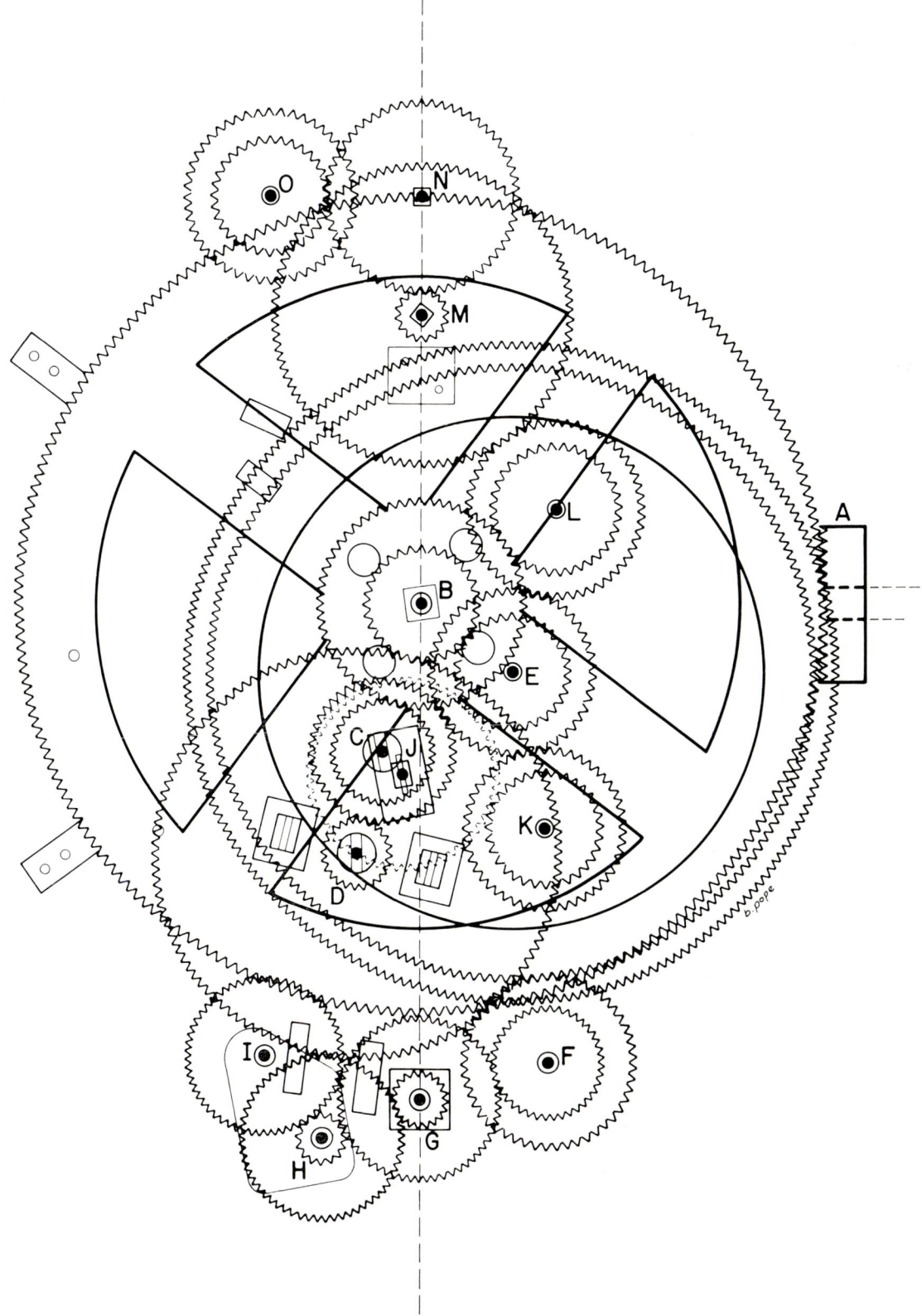

Fig. 29. General plan of all gearing, composite diagram.

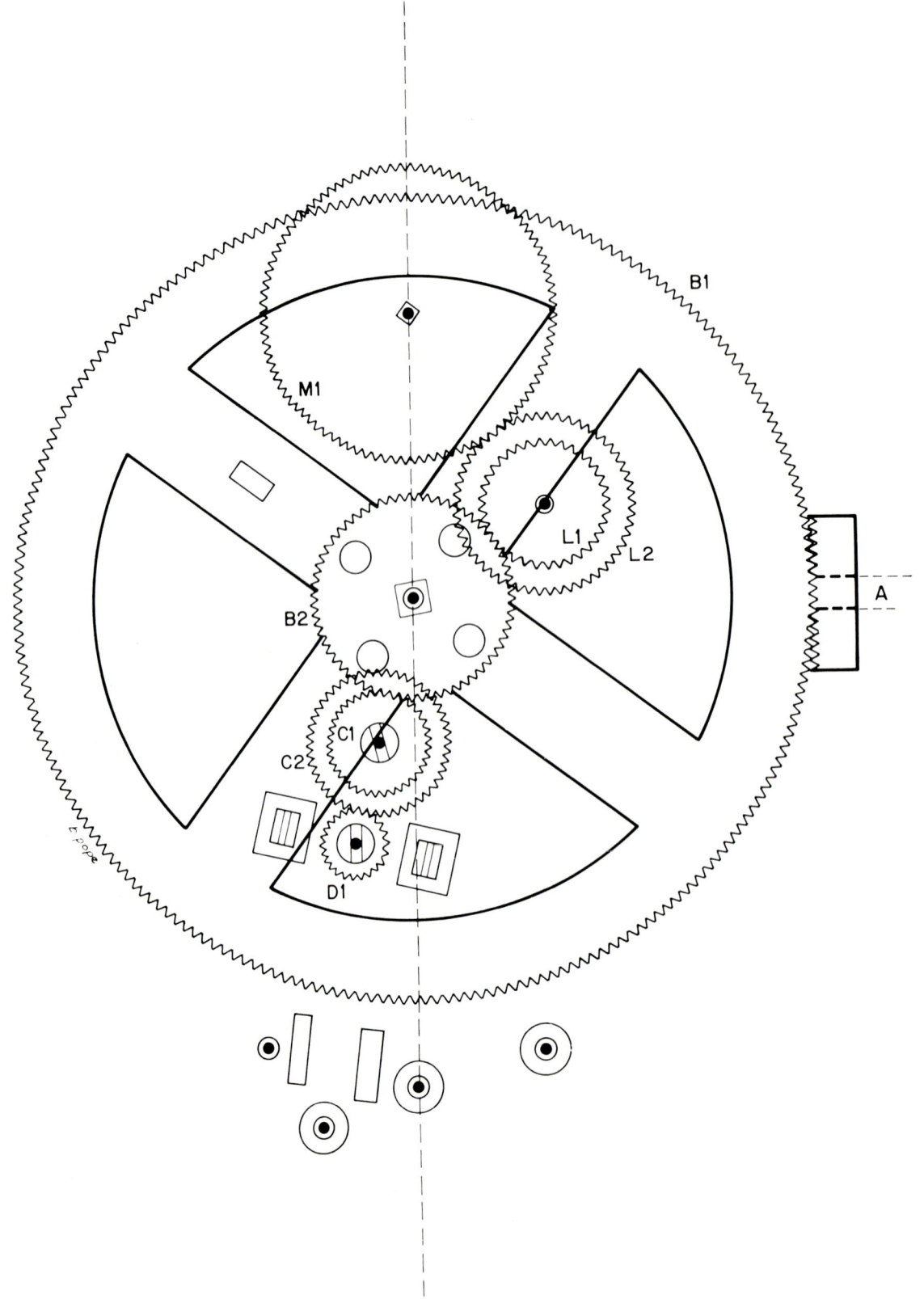

Fig. 30a. Gearing on front of main plate.

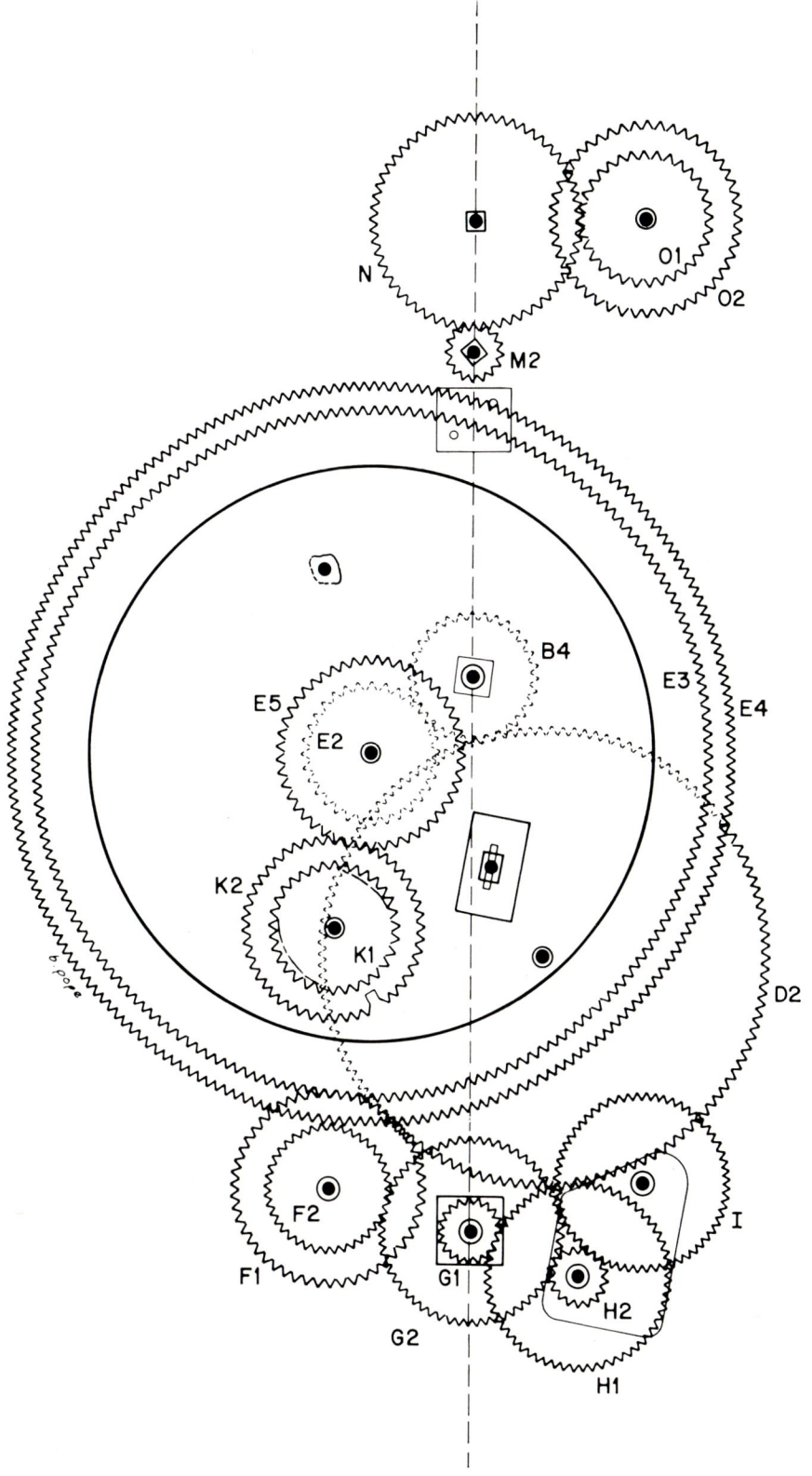

Fig. 30b. Gearing on back of main plate.

of the radius at six o'clock is inscribed a Greek letter Σ. We have therefore a subsidiary dial at this point, similar in construction to that over Gear I.

DESCRIPTION OF GEAR TRAINS

It is clear that the logical point of entry into the gearing system must be the main drive Wheel $B1$ and the contrate Gear A which feeds it. The sturdy construction of the drive wheel, its larger than usual teeth, and its placing at the join of the two central axes of the main surviving fragment all show that this prominent feature was intended as the basis for the entire construction. This is confirmed by the fact that the axis serves as a center for two separate gear systems in addition to the two pinion drives from here to the center of the differential turntable which is the central prominent feature of the other side of the main base plate.

Since the main drive wheel sits directly below and concentric with the front dial plate with its annual and zodiac circle divisions it is reasonable to suppose that this wheel is to have an annual rotation associated with it. This does not imply that the wheel is to be turned by waterpower or by hand or some other means at an actual rate of one turn during a year, but rather that a turn of this wheel is to "represent" a year, no matter what rate at which it may be turned. If the circular drum now fixed by calcification to the underside of the one surviving fragment of the back dial (Svoronos, fragment B) is a crank handle, as I suppose, then the device is to be turned by hand. It might then be used by adjusting it to past and future dates to calculate by means of the gearing the various astronomical and calendrical phenomena. Alternatively it might be moved step by step, adjusting it currently a day at a time so that each day it would give the phenomena for the present. If the drum is not such a handle, but a moon indicator or some other part of the dial machinery, then it is open to question whether the mechanism was designed to be turned in one of these ways by a handle or whether it was made to be moved automatically, perhaps in conjunction with a clepsydra and possibly, too, an anaphoric clock arrangement that would show the phenomena associated with the daily rotation of the heavens. Exactly such a device could well have been associated with the sort of display which has been suggested as a restoration for the well-known Tower of Winds built by Andronicus Kyrrhestes in Athens in the second quarter of the first century B.C. It is almost certainly, however, not this particular piece of mechanism, for the Tower of Winds is essentially a Roman construction, with the wind names inscribed in Roman letters, but the Antikythera mechanism inscriptions are Greek, though of much the same period.

It takes approximately, or perhaps exactly, five turns of the contrate wheel to produce a single turn of the

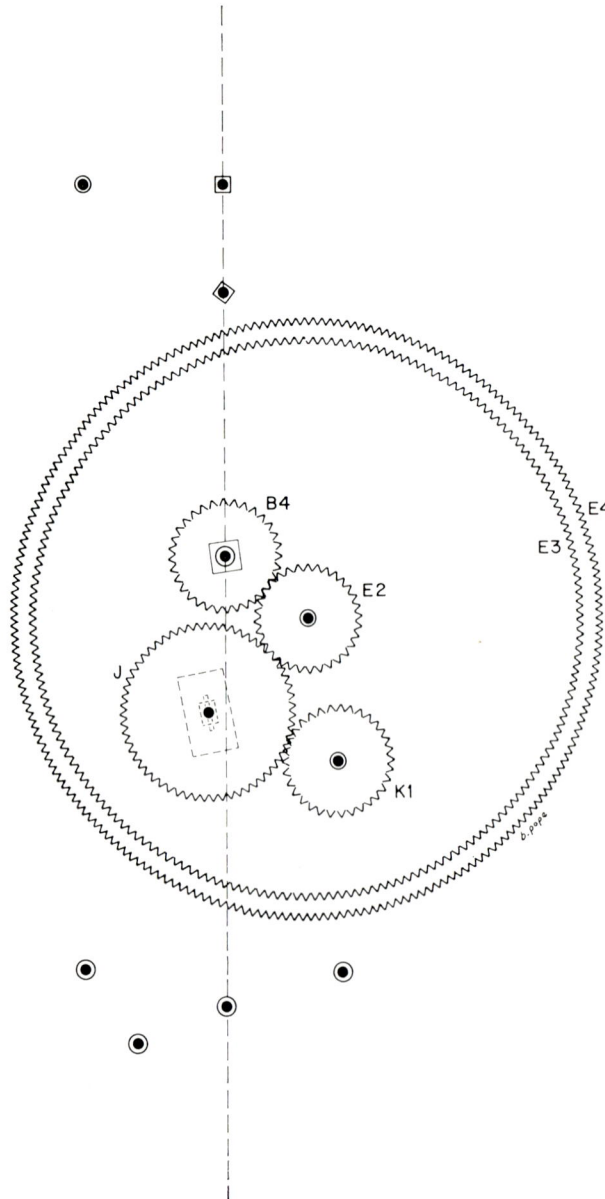

FIG. 31. Gearing on back of differential turntable.

The measured distance between centers O and N is 25.8 mm corresponding to about 103 teeth; therefore, if a wheel on axis O is to mesh with the 64-tooth wheel at N, it must have ca. 39 teeth. I conjecture that one may have in fact a gearing of $64/32 = 2/1$, the level of both wheels being just above the back surface of the main plate. This is in agreement with evidence from the main fragment that leads one to suppose that there is a space of about 12.5 mm between the inner surfaces of the main base plate and the back dial plate.

On the outer surface of the dial plate, around this axis, a circle of ca. 9 mm radius is inscribed. It has a pair of perpendicular diameters which lie in the directions of the main axes of the base plate, and to the left drive wheel. A turn of the contrate corresponds therefore to about 73 days and if the presumed crank handle drum were graduated in days around its edge such graduations would be about 2.6 mm apart, some 70 per cent larger than the normal separation between gear teeth.

The association of the main wheel with an annual cycle is strengthened by consideration of the relation of this wheel to the differential turntable. Though the complex that is formed by the Gears $E1/B3$ and $E2/B4$ is extremely difficult to see visually or on the radiographs it seems to agree best with the existing four identical gears of 32 teeth each whose function is only to transmit two motions from the main drive wheel to the differential. One motion is that of the drive wheel subjected to only a single 1/1 gear ratio that leaves it at the same annual rate but reverses the direction of rotation. The other goes through the train $B2 - C1 + C2 - D1 + D2 - B4 - E2$ which introduces successively ratios of approximately 3/2, 2/1, and 4/1 as well as four reversals of direction. There feeds into the differential turntable therefore an annual motion and another which goes round approximately twelve times during a year.

It seems that the function of the turntable must be to take these two rates of revolution, one annual and the other approximately monthly, and compound them either as a sum or a difference. The two obvious and almost inescapable astronomical choices would be associated with the fact that the synodic motion of the Moon—the cycle of the phases from New Moon to Full Moon—is the difference between the siderial motions of the Sun and of the Moon against the backdrop of the fixed stars. The Sun appears to rotate through the stars of the zodiac in about 365 days while the Moon changes place in a period of about $27\frac{1}{3}$ days and changes through its cycle of phases in about $29\frac{1}{2}$ days.

Either the differential turntable adds the revolutions of the Sun to those of the synodic phenomena to produce the revolutions of the Moon, or it subtracts the revolutions of the Sun from those of the Moon to produce the cycles of the synodic months. From the fact that $B3$ and $B4$ rotate in opposite directions (and so therefore do $E1$ and $E2$) it follows that it is the latter case which applies. This is confirmed by the gear ratios (see p. 45) which introduce numbers compatible with the classical Greek calendrical device of the Metonic cycle in which 19 solar years are made to correspond exactly with 235 lunations and therefore with 254 siderial revolutions of the Moon. The gearing contains wheels that correspond very well with the prime numbers of 19 and 127 which are needed to mechanize the Metonic cycle. We have in fact

$$\frac{64}{38} \times \frac{48}{24} \times \frac{127}{32} = \frac{254}{19}$$

so that the differential gear is fed with 254 revolutions

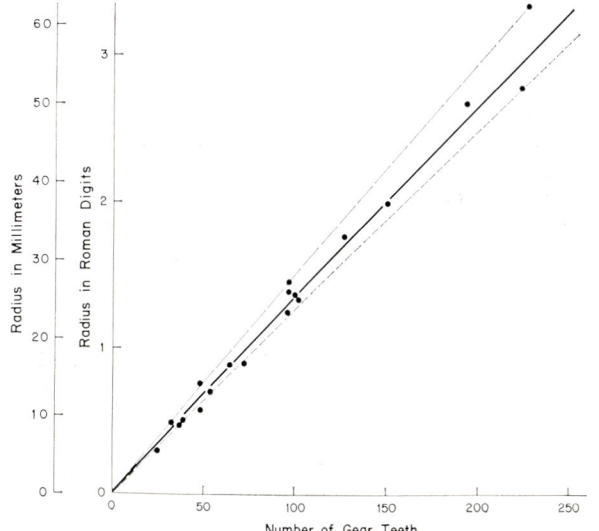

FIG. 32. Number of gear teeth as a function of wheel radius. The upper, middle and lower straight lines correspond respectively to 4.44, 4.00, and 3.75 gear teeth per mm radius, or diametral pitches of 0.45, 0.50 and 0.53 mm diameter per tooth.

of $E2$ and 19 reverse revolutions of $E1$ for every 19 (direct) turns of the main drive wheel; this produces 235/2 revolutions of the whole differential turntable and all the gears mounted upon it.

Though the evidence might be considered weak because of the difficulties already stated in estimating precisely the number of gear teeth on each wheel, it becomes stronger when one takes into account the number-theoretic restraints which exist. For example, if instead of the 19-year Metonic cycle we had supposed as a basis for the train the corresponding numbers for the 8-year Octoëteris, it would have been necessary to produce an overall ratio of 99 synodic months and therefore 107 siderial revolutions of the Moon to 8 of the Sun. This might have been achieved by a set of gears yielding

$$\frac{64}{32} \times \frac{48}{24} \times \frac{107}{32} = \frac{107}{8}$$

For the first two ratios it would have been possible for any pair of gears to be used with a simple 2/1 ratio, but whatever the arrangement it is inescapable that somewhere in the train there should be a wheel having the large prime number 107 or a multiple of it as its gear tooth count. There is no such wheel in the train since those that exist are either far too big or far too small, however generously one supposes the possible errors to accumulate. It is therefore impossible for the gear train to be a mechanization of the Octoëteris.

Similar conclusions are obtained if one attempts to force the existing evidence into the other readily available alternatives for some sort of year/month ratio. All ratios involving the numbers of days in such period contain inadmissible prime factors; 365 days implies the presence of a wheel with $73n$ teeth, and $365\frac{1}{4}$

TABLE 3

Synoptic Table of Gear Wheels and Inter-axial Distances

Number of teeth	
15	$H2$
16	$M2$
20	$G1$
24	$D1$—5.4 mm
30	$F2$
32	$E1$—9.0 mm, $B3$, $B4$, $E2$, $K1$, $O1$
36	$L1$—8.7 mm
38	$C1$—9.3 mm
48	$C2$—10.6 mm, A—13.9 mm, $E5$, $F1$, $K2$, $O2$
54	$L2$—13.0 mm
60	$G2$, $H1$, I
63	N
64	$B2$—16.4 mm, J
72	CD—16.6 mm
96	$M1$—23.3 mm, EK—27.2 mm, EJ—26.0 mm
100	BL—25.6 mm
102	BC—25.0 mm
127	$D2$—ca. 33.0 mm
150	LM—37.4 mm
192	$E3$—50.2 mm
222	$E4$—52.4 mm
225?	$B1$—63.0 mm

The best fit is approximately 4 teeth for every 1 mm of radius, i.e., ca. 1.57 mm/tooth.

days implies an impossibly large factor of 487. A month of $29\frac{1}{2}$ days would require a wheel of $59n$ teeth, and a siderial month of $27\frac{1}{3}$ days requires one of the $41n$ teeth, and all these seem contradicted by the gear count estimates.

It should be noted, however, that if by some device the direction of rotation of one of the movements could be reversed so that the inputs to the differential turntable were the solar year and the synodic month and the output the siderial month, we could use a train quite close to that attested to produce an acceptable synodic month, viz.:

$$\frac{64}{38} \times \frac{47}{25} \times \frac{125}{32} = \frac{235}{19}$$

I cannot, however, see any easy way in which a small change of gearing would permit this use of the turntable, and, much stronger than this, the alternative just proposed would then give a far less logical arrangement of the dial plates. The synodic month would then be shown with the solar year in the top dial, and the lower back dial would then show on a dial graduated with ca. 60 divisions the passage of the Moon around the zodiac and every twelve such complete revolutions. It does not seem to make sense astronomically, so we return to the sole remaining conjecture that the turntable has an input of the two siderial revolutions and an output of the synodic month.

It has already been remarked that in this particular train of gears a further restriction on gear tooth numbers is introduced by the fact that the train begins and ends at the B axis of the mechanism. Because of this, the sum of the radii and therefore that of the teeth in the Gears $B2$, $C1$, $C2$, and $D1$ should be equal to the sum of $D2$ and $B4$. If we assume that the wheels on the drive shaft are already given at the sizes of 64 and 32 teeth by ease of division, and that the wheels of 38 and 127 teeth are determined by the prime factors in the required ratio, this leaves a total of 57 teeth in which a ratio of 2/1 must be achieved. Though the exact solution is 38/19 it would reduce in effect to having the gear pair $C1 + C2$ become an idler gear of 38 teeth—or any number, say 36 or 40 for that matter—and leaving the essential prime number 19 to be produced by a pinion of that number of teeth at $D1$. This has been rejected in favor of a solution of 48/24 using a larger number of teeth noticeably smaller than those elsewhere in the mechanism. I think that the motivation has been quite simply the avoidance of that pinion of 19 which would have been difficult to cut and quite uneven in its operation, but in any event the laying out of this particular gear train demonstrates the need for much sophistication in design.

It is noteworthy that the almost collinear axes BCD have been placed along a line that is inclined at about 14° to the main axis of the mechanism instead of direct on it. So far as I can see this has been dictated by the need to enable the perimeter of the large Gear $D2$ to clear the supports of the gear system on axes F, G, H, and I which underlie the center of the lower back dial. If so this is again a considerable feat in sophisticated design since an axis on the front of the main plate has had to be located so as to produce a clearance at the back of this plate.

It is, I think, worth while to compare the gear ratios used here with those of the only other known specimens, those of the text by al-Biruni (ca. 1000 A.D.) [15] and of a geared calendar contained in an astrolabe, now in the Museum of the History of Science in Oxford (Gunther No. 5) made by Muhammad b. Abi Bakr b. Muhammad ar-Rashidi al-Ibari al-Isfahani in A. H. 618 = 1221/2 A.D. which follows the same general plan as the text. Biruni uses a gear train which may be written as

$$48 - 24 + 59 - 19 + 59 - 7 + 10 - 40$$

in which the double pinion $7 + 10$ is turned once a week and produces a revolution of the wheel of 40 in the 28 days of the siderial month. The wheels of 19 +

---

[15] Eilhard Wiedemann, "Ein Instrument, das die Bewegung von Sonne und Mond darstellt, nach al Biruni," *Der Islam* **4** (1913): pp. 5-13. I have published notes on the text and the astrolabe in my "Origin of Clockwork, Perpetual Motion and the Compass," see n. 24, p. 43. It may now be noted that Biruni ascribes the work to a Nastulus (or Bastulus) who is now identified as the (Syrian) maker of the earliest known dated (A.H. 315 = 927/8 A.D.) astrolabe. See Alain Brieux, Paris, Catalogue, November, 1973: pp. 6-9.

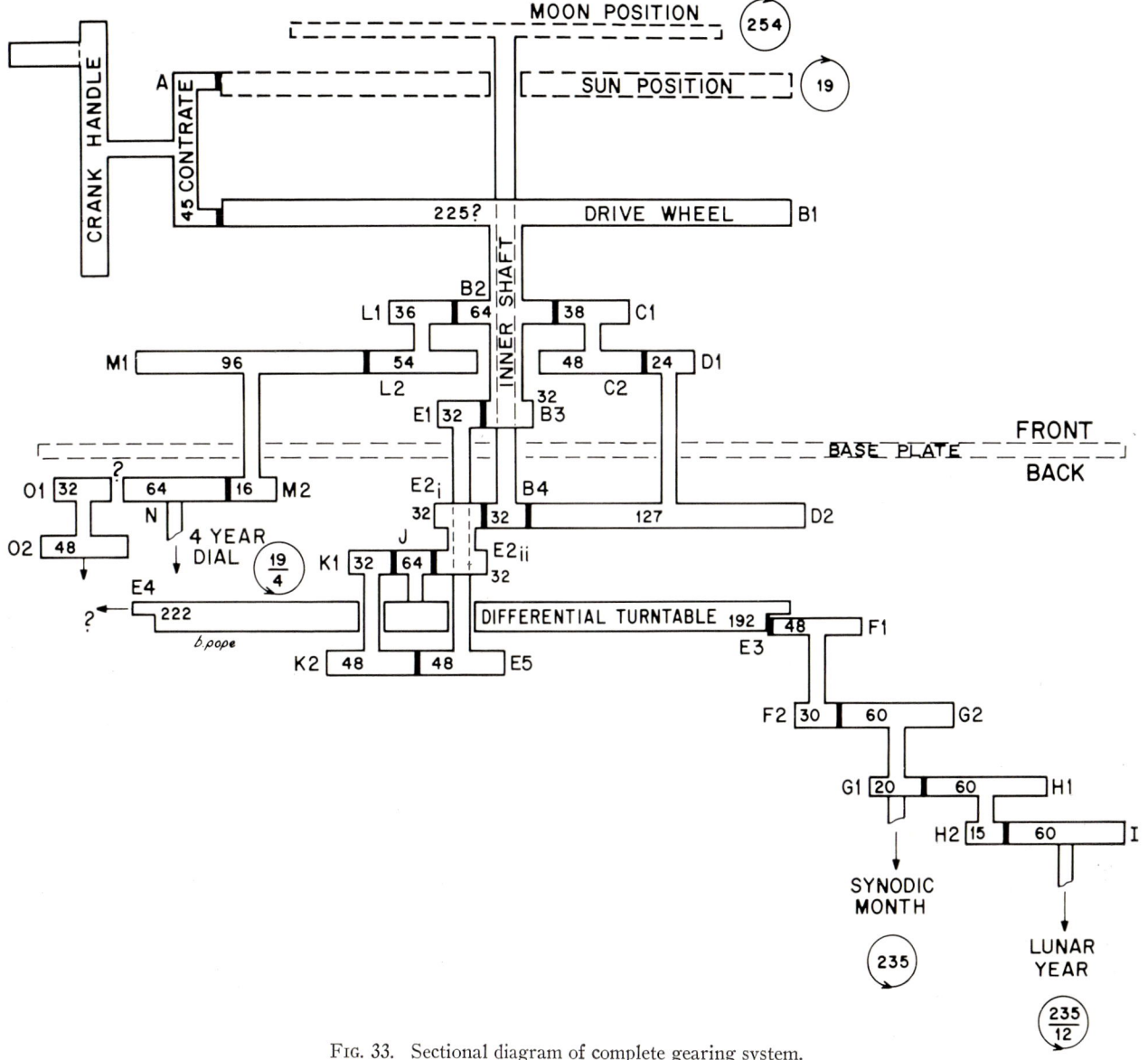

Fig. 33. Sectional diagram of complete gearing system.

59 rotate in a double month of 59 days and carry a moon phase volvelle with day numbers 1 to 29 and 1 to 30 alternately as well as an ingenious arrangement of a pair of black circles and a pair of silvered circles which can be viewed through a window to give the images of Full Moon and New Moon. The gearing then continues to make the wheel of 48 teeth rotate just 236 times in 19 months, a tolerable but not very good approximation for the Metonic cycle. A small modification would have given a much better result, $viz.$: $47 - 24 + 60 - 19 \ldots$ which yields a ratio of 235/19. Biruni gives two other alternative systems, one of which makes the year not solar, but a lunar one of exactly 12 synodic months and another which seems too corrupted to make sense.

In the astrolabe which very significantly is constructed with equilateral triangular teeth just like those of the Antikythera fragments, the gearing system is

$$60 - 10 + 64 - 64 + 64 - 8 + 13 - 48$$

except that the original pinion of 8 teeth has been replaced by a more modern one with 10 teeth. The system is that the wheels of 64 teeth rotate in a double month and carry a Moon phase dial with the day numbers as before. The wheel of 48 then rotates 13 times in 12 months and therefore shows the siderial month, and the wheel of 60 teeth rotates once in 12 months and shows therefore the lunar year. There is no indication for the solar year, and the calendar is therefore completely lunar and Islamic.

In both cases, however, there are gear trains which produce calendrical ratios of the months and the years comparable to those of the Antikythera mechanism and in one case using also the Metonic cycle, though in a more simple fashion. It seems quite clear that the tradition of the geared calendrical work must have been continued from Greco-Roman times to Islam even though there are no other texts now known. Arabic material in this area is not too well published, however, so it is always possible that more traces will be uncovered in due course.

The remaining gear system proceeding from the main drive wheel is that which leads to the upper back dial through the train $B2 - L1 + L2 - M1 + M2 - N$, it being remembered that the last named gear wheel is restored to this place only conjecturally from its place on the dial plate fragment (Svoronos, fragment C). If this part of the reconstruction is correct, and the gear tooth counts are approximately correct also we have the implied ratio

$$\frac{64}{36} \times \frac{54}{96} \times \frac{16}{63} = \frac{16}{63}$$

from which it follows that the main part of the upper back dial corresponds to a revolution approximately every four years.

My first conjecture was that the above ratio led the way either to a dial exhibiting the period of the planets or to one based upon the 223-month eclipse cycle which is referred to in part of the inscription on the instrument door panels. For the first alternative a dial plate inscribed in the 360° of the zodiac rather than the 47 or 48 divisions actually found would have been much more appropriate and, moreover, one would have to assume that quite large numbers of gears to produce the required ratios for the periods of the planets are now lacking. For the latter period one would have to assume that somewhere in the gear train there should appear a wheel with the prime number of 223 teeth, and this is clearly not so.

Taking the approximately four-year period and the dial division into 47 or 48 parts together, one is led to suppose that what is indicated must be the months of this cycle, either synodic or calendar. If it is the synodic month which is involved, the full 235 months of the cycle might well have been divided up into 5 sections of 47 each, and in that case the gear train would be required to make 5 revolutions during 19 of the main drive wheel. This could have been achieved by some such a set of ratios as

$$\frac{64}{36} \times \frac{50}{95} \times \frac{18}{64} = \frac{5}{19}$$

which seems also within tolerable limits for the observed tooth counts.

We find, therefore, that this train could bear the interpretation either of a 4-year cycle or of one of 47 synodic months. The former would give an exact number of days, 1,461, for a complete cycle and these would be divided up into 48 (Egyptian) months of 30 days each together with the four sets of epagomenal days, three of the sets being of 5 days and the fourth of 6 days. Five such concentric scales would contain 20 solar years, so that the fifth ring would not be completely used if only the months of the 19-year cycle were inscribed. Presumably each calendar month would be inscribed with the dates of New Moon and Full Moon at that place in the cycle.

For the latter alternative, the dial would be inscribed with divisions corresponding to the 47 synodic months on each of the 5 rings, and in each division would be inscribed the dates of New Moon and Full Moon as before. The former alternative seems to me slightly more to be preferred from the evidence of the gearing, the latter more suitable to the exhibiting of calendrical data by the entire mechanism. It seems to me that only a much more certain gear count or a better reading of the dial fragments could enable us to choose between these two alternatives or, indeed, to be quite sure that the intention of the dial is something else quite different.

The analysis of the remaining gearing leading to the small subsidiary dial at the upper back seems to me quite hopeless at this stage. The only clues are the very poorly preserved remains of gears $O1 + O2$, and the four divisions and inscribed letter Σ on the small dial itself. I cannot even guess as to whether $O1$ is intended to mesh with N or with another gear coaxial with N. The expectations from astronomical or calendrical theory do not help much either. It would seem futile to introduce a gear train to convert this 4-year cycle back to one of a single year subdivided by the dial into four seasons, it would also seem absurd to introduce a 1/1 gearing so that the four separate years could be shown on the subsidiary dial. If the 4-year cycle is to be geared up to a larger period, then depending on the two choices already given for interpreting the main dial, one would expect that either the indicated cycle should be 19 solar years or the 47 synodic months should be geared up to a Metonic cycle of 235 or an eclipse cycle of 223 synodic months. This latter is the most likely possibility, corresponding to almost one complete turn of the Moon's nodes with respect to the zodiac or exactly 19 turns of them with respect to the synodic month cycle of the lower back dial. In none of these cases would the four-part division of this subsidiary dial seem appropriate, and the last alternative, though most attractive, seems to be ruled out by the absence of any gear wheel large enough to have the prime number of 223 teeth.

The differential turntable is certainly the most spectacular mechanical feature of the Antikythera device because of its extreme sophistication and lack of any historical precedent. Since it lies to one side of the central line of the back of the main plate and is overlaid by two dials, attested by surviving fragments and leaving no space between, it is impossible that the turntable should be just a display device involving perhaps some epicyclic gearing to illustrate planetary motions. There is no room for any such display, and the turntable and dials are quite clearly preserved very near their original positions. Furthermore there seems enough of the gearing to provide the turntable with a pair of (opposite) inputs corresponding to the solar and lunar siderial revolutions, and an output which readily bears interpretation as that which should be provided by such a differential gear arrangement. Thus even though one must presume the existence of the Gear J which is now lacking, it seems quite secure to interpret the structure in this way.

From its design (see fig. 34) it is clear that the differential turntable must turn at a rate which is given by half the difference (i.e. half the algebraic sum) of its two inputs. In this case the output will be half the $254 - 19 = 235$ synodic revolutions of the Moon which take place during the 19-year Metonic cycle. It would have been possible to obtain immediately an output with one turn per synodic month by leading the revolution off from the turntable by a 2/1 ratio produced by a wheel having just half as many teeth as that around the rim of the turntable, that is by a wheel of 96 teeth engaging with the 192 of Gear $E3$ for example. Such a large wheel, however, would have prevented subsequent gearing from coming near to its axis, and instead the route has been taken of using a train of smaller wheels that first give a $192/48 = 4/1$ ratio with the turntable rotation and then decrease it again $30/60 = 1/2$.

I suppose that the use of 30/60 instead of the 32/64 used elsewhere in the gearing is motivated by the fact that the next part of the train derives a 1/12 ratio by reductions in two stages of 1/3 and 1/4. By using a gear of 60 teeth as a basis one is enabled to employ pinions of 20 and 15 teeth, whereas with a wheel of 64 teeth the 1/3 ratio would become impossible. The entire train then, starting with $F2$, is based upon wheels of 60 teeth.

It is worth special note that the Axis F occupies a position to the left of the main dial center G and slightly above it, quite symmetrical with the Axis I to the right of center. The Axis I is the center for the subsidiary dial which shows a revolution in 12 of the months indicated singly by the main dial, presumably, therefore, giving indications for a lunar year. One might reasonably expect that Axis F would therefore also be a center for a subsidiary dial, presumably one connected with its revolution at the rate of two turns per synodic month. I see, however, no trace of such a dial even though the surface of the plate is well preserved at this point. Furthermore the end of the axle does not appear to be squared, and there seems no obvious calendrical or astronomical function for such a half-month cycle.

In connection with the Axis F it is also possible that there might have been another gear rotating on this center quite independently of Gears $F1$ and $F2$, and meshing with $E4$. Such a gear would have had to have

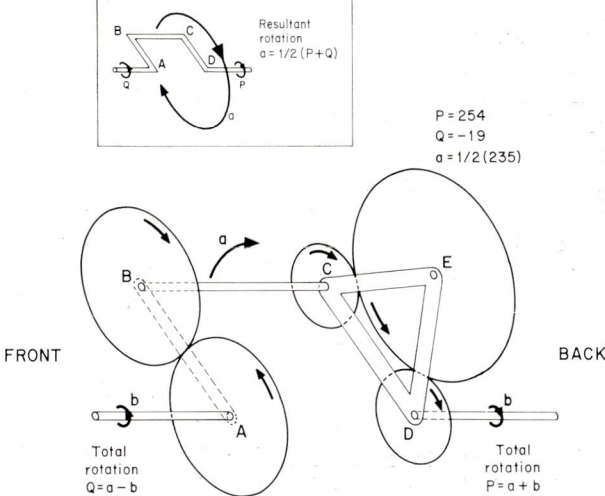

Fig. 34. Principle of the differential gear system.

about 40 teeth, intermediate in size between $F1$ and $F2$, and it would have produced a ratio of ca. 22/40 with the differential output and therefore led to a rotation in ca. 0.36 months or 10.6 days. Again, I find no radiographic evidence to support such a conjecture and no reasonable function for a dial indicating a rotation at any such rate. We assume, therefore, that this lower back dial has a central feature indicating the cycle through a single synodic month, and one subsidiary dial for the lunar year of twelve months.

If, however, the Gear $E4$, which looks as if it should be one of the two chief outputs from the elaborate differential turntable, does not mesh in this fashion, its purpose is a mystery. I can see no way for $E4$ to mesh with any other gearing in the neighborhood of this lower back dial where surely a revolution based somehow on synodic months would belong.

The upper and lower back dials between cover so much of the surface of the back dial plate that there seems little space left over for other indications. The base plate all around the turntable is so complete that one can say with some certainty that there exists no axle hole or gear mounting that could serve as a basis for transmitting a motion from somewhere near the perimeter of $E4$ to the front side of the mechanism and thence to some indication near the front dial system.

The only possibility I can see is that $E4$ was arranged to feed to the upper back dial system from some axis lying outside the range of the extant fragments. The most reasonable axis for this would be that of a subsidiary dial placed to the left of the main dial Axis N, symmetrical to that of O to the right. A single gear on the axis, by virtue of the radius required, would have ca. 125 teeth, and would produce a rotation therefore in 250/222 months. This could conceivably have something to do with the anomalistic month or with the motion of the nodes associated with the eclipse cycle, but I regard any such suggestions as extremely insecure pending further evidence from the gearing and dial system after cleaning or other examination. It should be noted that in any gearing of the type suggested the 222 teeth of E4 could not be associated with the 223 months of the eclipse cycle for the factor goes the wrong way around. For such an eclipse cycle one would need a wheel of some multiple of 223 teeth actuated in effect at the rate of one tooth per month. Here the 222 teeth are subdivision of a single month, or rather of a two-month period. The numerical similarity seems therefore to be nothing more than a coincidence.

THE INSCRIPTIONS

GENERAL DESCRIPTION OF THE STATE OF THE FRAGMENTS

The fragments, as seen during the present studies, consist principally of the decomposition products of the bronze machine, squeezed together under great pressure, corroded by sea water, and covered with calcareous accretions. In some places the material appears compact and hard, and in such it seems likely that some free metal exists at the core. In many other places the material is so powdery and friable that it cannot support its own weight, and crumbles under the least provocation in spite of the early treatment with polyvinyl acetate or cellulose nitrate or some such consolident. Such crumbling has markedly reduced the size of all fragments, as may be seen by comparing old photographs with more recent views. Some of the

TABLE 4

A POSSIBLE PARAPEGMA SCHEME BASED UPON THE EUDOXOS DATA IN GEMINOS

Limb Fragment	A	Fall equinox	Libra 1
	B	Pleiades er	Libra 8
	Γ	Hyades er ?	Libra 22
	Δ	Arcturus es ?	Scorpio 8
	E	Pleiades ms	Scorpio 19
Preserved Portion	Z	Hyades ms	Scorpio 29
	H	Sirius ms or er	Sagitt 12 or 16
	Θ	Altair mr or es	Sagitt 26 or Capric 18
	I	Arcturus er or Spring equinox	Pisces 4 or Aries 1
	K	Pleiades es	Aries 13
	Λ	Hyades es	Aries 21
	M	Taurus rises	
	N	Vega er	Aries 27
	Ξ	Pleiades mr	Taurus 22
	O	Hyades mr	Gemini 5
	Π	Gemini rises	
	P	Altair er	Gemini 7
	Σ	Arcturus ms	Gemini 13
	T	Summer solstice	Cancer 1
	Υ	Sirius mr	Cancer 27
	Φ	Altair ms	Leo 5
	X	?	
	Ψ	?	
Limb	Ω	Arcturus mr	Virgo 19

er evening rising
mr morning rising
es evening setting
ms morning setting

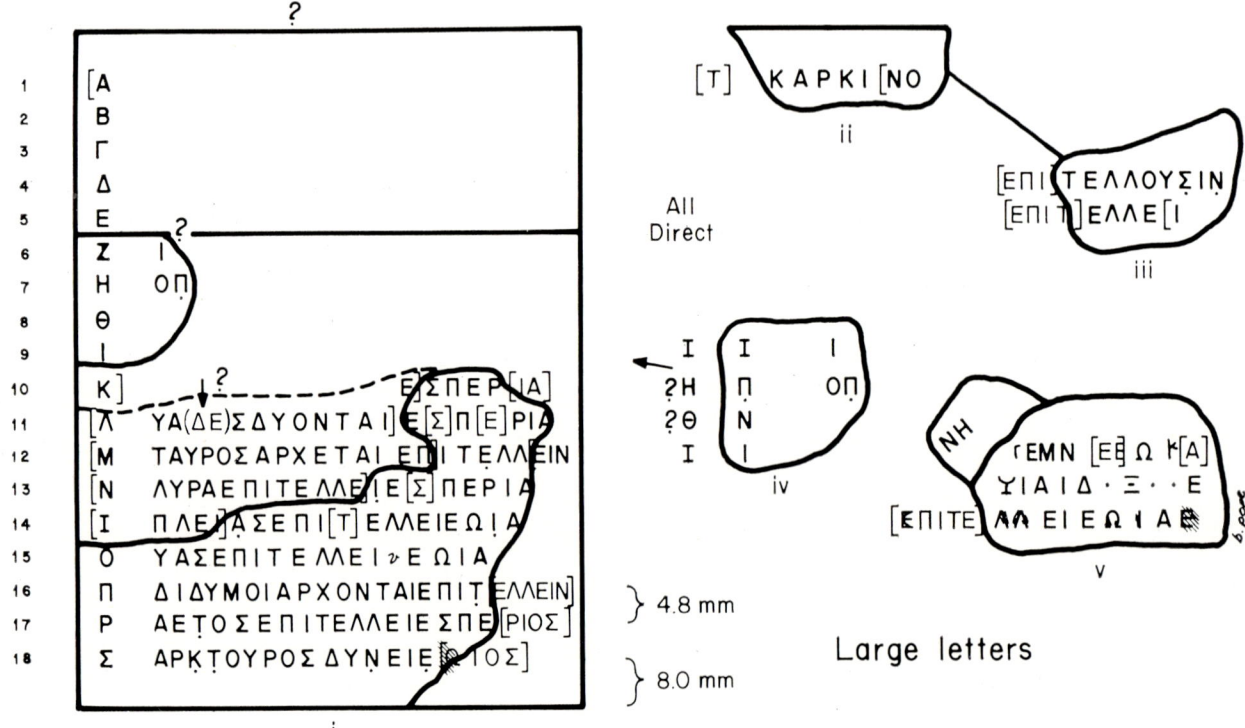

Fig. 35. Parapegma inscription.

changes have been due to the masterly separation of layers one from another at the hands of the museum technicians, but other changes represent a complete loss of evidence. Fortunately, in many cases of such loss there is the compensation that decay of a superficial layer has revealed new evidence on an underlying surface previously hidden from view. Because of this, the evidence of a complete set of photographs taken through the years has been particularly valuable to these studies, and I must thank the museum authorities, the late Dr. Ernst Zinner, and the Bayerische Staatsbibliothek at Munich for making them available.

As a curious effect of corrosion under pressure, it happens that one of the largest inscriptions, formerly on the back door of the instrument, though lost, all but for one small fragment, is preserved over a much larger area as a mirror-image inscription, scarcely blurred by its mode of formation, is quite legible on two of the main fragments and matches completely the direct inscription of the small piece of original door plate. It is, however, somewhat fragile, pieces of it having already been rubbed away, and any future cleaning would necessarily destroy it completely in revealing detail of the surfaces on which it is deposited.

In color the fragments range from the pale whitish green of Cassiterite [16] (stannic oxide) through all darker shades of the green and blue-green of Atacamite (basic cupric chloride), with an occasional patch of yellow-brown iron (?) accretion and some streaks of gray and gray-black over small areas. It is easy to see from inspection that the joins between fragments, when correctly made, give a good match of color patterns over the area of the join. This was found most helpful when I confirmed in 1961 the joins between the three main fragments which had been proposed on the basis of shape and configuration alone after the first examination some two years previously.

The four main fragments of the machine, as now preserved, are obviously identical with those lettered A, B, C, and D in the plates illustrating the original publication by Svoronos, though, as noted, they have been somewhat reduced in size by wear and by restoration in which accreted debris has been removed and plates separated from the cohering masses. I hope that, now that this investigation is published and the present evidence recorded, it may be judged possible and expeditious to continue the cleaning and separation particularly of the dial fragments with their crucial inscriptions. Fragment B of Svoronos has been markedly reduced in size by the removal in pieces, later reassembled, of an inscribed plate that was once the front door of the instrument. In addition to the three main fragments and this front door plate there exist some fifteen small fragments, most of them being scraps of

[16] These two minerals are the characteristic corrosion products of bronze. I thank Dr. A. E. Werner of the British Museum Laboratories for these identifications.

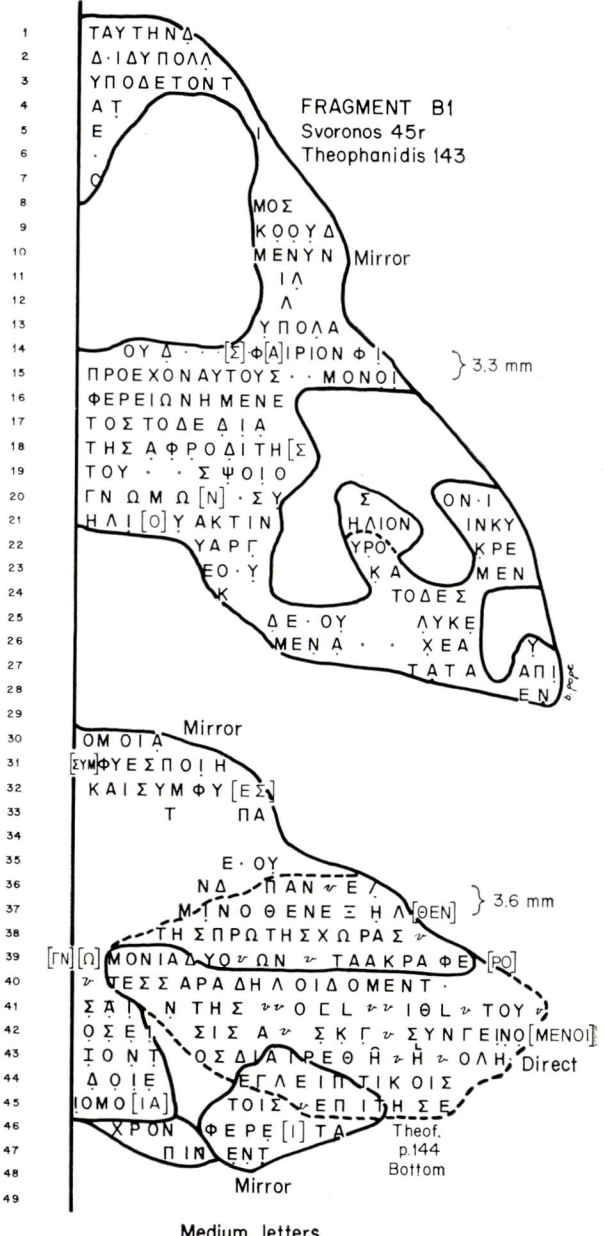

Fig. 36. Back door plate inscription.

inscribed plate which have been read and joined whenever possible. Fortunately it happens that the three chief inscriptions are in very different letter sizes and line separations, and on this basis it has been possible to classify each fragment and make some joins. In addition to these identifiable larger fragments, there is a little cardboard box, some 9 cm × 7 cm containing about 2 cm³ of tiny pieces and dust from which the chemical and metallurgical samples were provided.

The inscriptions all appear to be made by the same hand, but in three different sizes; large for the parapegma plates (interlinear distance 4.8 mm), medium

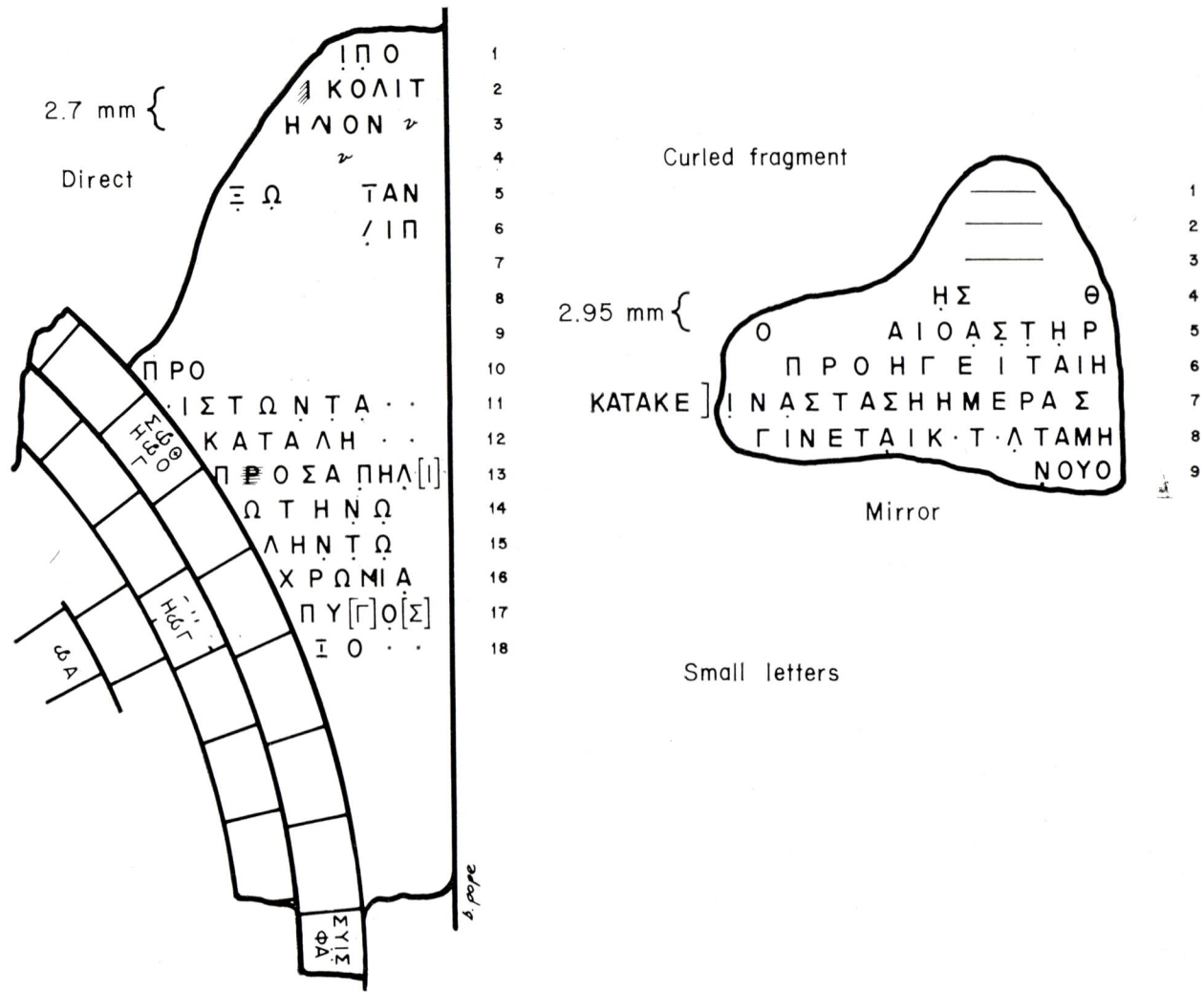

Fig. 37. Lower back dial inscription.

for the direct and mirror inscriptions from the back door (interlinear 3.3–3.6 mm), and small for the inscriptions around the back dials and on the front door (interlinear 2.6–2.9 mm).

The inscription is difficult to read and the material too delicate for squeezes or molds. Moreover, there are only two places in which photography has proved sufficient to give the forms of the letters sufficiently well for reproduction (see figs. 18, 39). Only in the second case, alas, do the photographs give nearly as much opportunity as the original for reading the text. From these it will appear that the epigraphical evidence strongly supports the dating of the wreck and machine. The letter forms are, in the opinion of Professor Benjamin Meritt, characteristic of the first century B.C., or more loosely, of Augustan times. For example, the left vertical of Π is much longer than the right; the vertical strokes of M and the horizontal ones of Σ are not parallel. There are tiny serifs at the end of each stroke (see fig. 39). This evidence is of some importance, for it shows agreement of the inscription in date, both by epigraphy and by content, with that of the wreck itself on archaeological grounds and on a possible astronomical dating of the calendar inscribed on the instrument scales. Thus the inscription certainly belongs with the instrument and its gears, and the whole assembly comes from the same period of the wreck and is no accidental later addition on top of the wreck. Even if a second ship had dropped overboard a nineteenth-century planetarium inscribed in Greek and of this curious and unfamiliar design (see page 12), it is unlikely that it would have been inscribed archaically in a first-century B.C. hand, and closely related to an ancient calendar.

The inscriptions are given in figures 35–38 using the normal epigraphic conventions where a dot under a letter indicates a doubtful reading and square brackets [ ] are used to enclose restored sections. Unfortunately there are only two sections, the large piece of parapegma plate and the lower section of the back door, where the preserved text is sufficiently extensive and coherent to read and understand more than a scattered word or two.

THE PARAPEGMA INSCRIPTION

There are preserved on the large fragment the last nine lines of a column which reads [17] as follows:

```
[K]              . . . evening
[Λ]   The Hya[des se]t in the evening
 M    Taurus [be]gins to rise
[N]   Vega rises in the evening
 Ξ    [The Pleiad]es rise in the morning
 O    The Hyades rise in the morning
 Π    Gemini begins to rise
 P    Altair rises in the evening
 Σ    Arcturus sets in the [morning]
```

The format and content is very similar to that of the traditional Greek calendar, particularly to that appended to the *Isagoge* (Introduction to Astronomy) of Geminos who flourished in Rhodes. From a dating of the Isis festival in this text, it is deduced by Manitius [18] that he flourished about 77 B.C., roughly contemporary with the Antikythera shipwreck.[19] These calendars and others like them are based upon the heliacal risings and settings of the bright stars and the zodiacal constellations, and include also weather indications and other phenomena based upon the seasonal climate. The terminology of this fragment does not deviate from the standard except in the use of the rare form ΥΑΣ instead of ΥΑΔΕΣ for the Hyades.

Since we do not have dates corresponding to these phenomena but only the key letters marking them, there is little one can do by way of astronomical commentary. Table 4 gives a set of positions in the year, according to a zodiacal calendar, for a complete scheme of all four heliacal risings and settings for each of the stars mentioned to gather with Sirius which almost certainly must have been included. I have included also the equinoxes and the summer solstice as well as the rising of Gemini which is given in the text and the rising, probably of Taurus, which is probably to be restored in line M. Evidently, however, there are not quite enough lines to go round, even without more constella-

---

[17] The lines Λ, M, N have now only their last words visible. The transcription of the beginnings, identifying Hyades, Taurus, and Vega, are taken from the unpublished notes of Rehm referring to a state of Fragment C when more of the parapegma plate was intact. One cannot now check these readings. I have assumed the plural form for the Hyades, ΥΑΔΕΣ instead of the singular, as in line O.

[18] Manitius edition of *Isagoge*, pp. 263–266.

[19] Professor Otto Neugebauer has, however, pointed out to me that the calculation of Manitius is insecure and that closer consideration of the evidence from the date of the Isis festival points to a later date in the first century A.D., the first half being more likely than the later part. The parapegma calendar is, however, in origin pre-Hipparchian and much older than the calendrical exposition of the *Isagoge*.

tion risings or other bright stars, so possibly various phenomena were combined or omitted altogether.

Table 4 is therefore not to be considered as anything but a most tentative reconstruction. It does show that the natural phenomena are by no means distributed, but it does not account well for the concentration of the first four letters of the alphabet in Libra, if this reading of the divided limb is correct Furthermore, it cannot be quite satisfactory that the line Π should be sandwiched between O and P which bear the dates 5 Gemini and 7 Gemini in the lines which Geminos ascribes to Eudoxos. We would then have presumably a concentration of three phenomena in one short three-day stretch of calendar, so presumably the scheme used separates these dates rather more widely than that of Eudoxos. It is also remarkable, if Rehm's reading for line N is correct, that we have an evening rising of Vega (Lyra) but not the evening setting of Sirius which should fall on Taurus 4 according to Geminos. As a further difficulty I feel there is some indication that the phenomena fall too thickly in the first part of the alphabet but there are too few of them for the available letter in the second part. In other words there is some mismatch or misplacement I cannot understand between the places of the letters on the limb and those on the preserved section of calendar. The mismatch is uncertain and may be quite small, but the problem seems to be unresolvable with this little evidence.

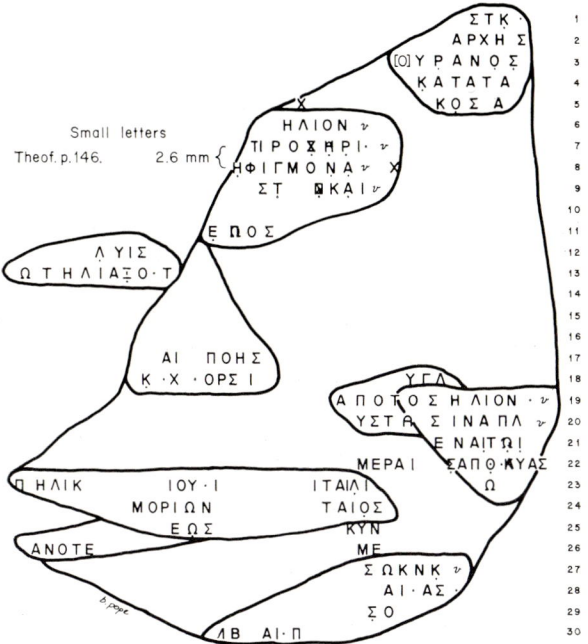

Fig. 38. Front door plate inscription.

Fig. 39a. Fragment containing lines 36-45 of back door inscription (see also fig. 40) oblique illumination.

Fig. 39b. Same fragment with direct illumination. This is the only place where more than a few inscribed letters can satisfactorily be photographed.

INSCRIPTIONS ON DOOR PLATES, AND MISCELLANEOUS

The largest piece of coherent and legible inscription is on the back door plate where we are able to make joins between mirror-image and direct incised characters on several fragments. I feel the following sections can be translated:

Line	
15	protruding
16	carries, of which one
17	and the other
18	[Venus]
⋮	
20	the pointer
21	the Sun's rays
⋮	
37	whence came out of
38	the first position
39	two pointers, whose ends carry
40	four, the one indicates
41	the 76 years., 19 yrs. of the
42	2[23] coming together
43	so that the whole will be divided
44	ecliptic
45	similar to those on the
46	carries

The readings in lines 18 and 42 are uncertain and conjectural, but in the latter I feel sure that the number is this rather than 235 which would be the alternative on astronomical grounds.

On the whole it seems that this text is concerned, as indeed it should be, with explaining the dials and pointer readings on the pair of back dials, and that these are based upon the Metonic and Callipic cycles of 19 years and 76 years, the former consisting of 235 months or 6,940 days, and the latter of 940 months or 27,759 days. The sign used for years in this passage, L, is that most common for the period, though elsewhere it may be used for the fraction ½. The number 223 occurring in line 42 refers of course to the cycle of 223 synodic months in which there occur 19 eclipse possibilities at either node.

In the inscription on the lower back dial (fig. 37) lines 13–14 might be read ΠΡΟΣ ΑΠΗΛ[Ι]ΩΤΗΝ, "Towards the East (wind)"; similarly perhaps lines 16–17 may be some form of ΙΑΠΥ[Γ]Ο[Σ], "west-

Fig. 40. Front door plate fragment with almost illegible inscription. See also fig. 22.

north-west (wind)" and line 6 some form of ΛΙΨ (genitive ΛΙΠΟΣ) "west-south-west (wind)." But what the point of these directional mentions may be I cannot guess.

THE ANTIKYTHERA MECHANISM AS AN HISTORICAL DOCUMENT

Even if the Antikythera fragments had been no more than a few small bronze wheels and gears of uncertain function, they would constitute an historical relic of enormous interest and importance. So little has come down to us from the Greek Miracle, decisive for the birth of our sort of civilization, that we have become used to making a great deal of the things we have. Preservation has been highly selective so that we tend to see the Greeks in terms of only the more indestructible masses of building stone, statuary, and ceramic together with coins and a few grave goods that are the main holdings of our museums and archaeological sites. Minor objects, especially those in non-precious metals are rare, and even when they are preserved by local cataclysm as in Pompeii and Herculaneum, objects of scientific interest almost never go beyond a few common weights and measures, perhaps the special tools of the local surgeon or dentist, and the calipers of the stonemason, builder, or carpenter. Wheels from carriages and carts survive from deep antiquity, but there is absolutely nothing but the Antikythera fragments that looks anything like a fine gear wheel or small piece of mechanism. Indeed the evidence for scientific instruments and fine mechanical objects is so scant that it is often thought that the Greeks had none. There is a whole apologetic used most energetically by Benjamin Farringdon that explains the (fictitious) total absence of Greek experimental sciences from literary remarks that the institution of slavery made manual work repugnant to the intellectual of those times and thereby created an unbridgeable gulf between the worlds of scientific theory and those of mechanics and technology. For an example of this one might cite the remarks of Plutarch that Archimedes for all his enormous skill

would not deign to leave behind him any commentary or writing on such subjects; but, repudiating as sordid and ignoble the whole trade of engineering, and every sort of art that lends itself to mere use and profit, he placed his whole affection and ambition in those purer speculations where there can be no reference to the vulgar needs of life....

At the least the tangible presence of this one complex scientific artifact gives the lie to an historical theory that has long been outworn and is now unworthy of serious consideration.

More generally, from the entire Greco-Roman period there is only one class of extant objects to illustrate the birth of modern science and mathematics, the sundials. There exist a precious few—in fact just eleven known examples—of small bronze plates engraved with a network of lines and inscriptions that enable the user to find the time of day from the position of the Sun.[20] There also exists a much larger, indeed a surprisingly large number of about 300 specimens, of larger marble blocks, shaped into spherical, conical, and other surfaces, and engraved with similar lines that may be used to tell the time of day, or perhaps more often, the season of the year.[21] From all these sundials one may learn a little of the history of our scientific culture that is not told from the surviving texts. Technologically there is nothing difficult about the cutting of the metal or the stone. It could be done, and regrettably often was, by the crudest artisans. All the art lay in the design of the lines, all the cleverness in designing an object that mirrored the motions of the heavens. It seems as if they were making little monuments to their cunning astronomical understanding rather than devising useful instruments for anything so mundane as to tell the time. This is not to say the sundials were never used—especially as one goes later into Roman times there is clear simplification and debasement in design and with it a move away from intellectual creation and towards function and utilitarianism. Here again though we may be prejudiced by selective survival. We are dealing, after all, only with those specimens that are monumental or decorative enough to have lasted. The useful time tellers may have been simple scratchings on stone walls, long since worn away or defaced.

To be classed with the sundials, however, is one especially remarkable survival. The Tower of Winds, located in the Roman Agora in the heart of Athens, was built by Andronicus Kyrrhestes of Macedonia about the second quarter of the first century B.C. It was a monument designed in accord with the science of the day with an especially complicated sundial on each face of its octagonal tower, a wind vane and a frieze of the gods of the prevailing winds above that, and a whole series of marvelous astronomical and probably other showpieces inside. It was, in fact, a sort of Zeiss planetarium of the classical world. Moreover, it is noteworthy as being one of the very few buildings from

---

[20] These have been collected and published in my paper, "Portable Sundials in Antiquity, including an Account of a New Example from Aphrodisias," *Centaurus* 14, 1 (1969): pp. 242–266.

[21] The corpus of all known examples has been fully cataloged and annotated by Sharon L. Gibbs, "*Greek and Roman Sundials,*" Ph.D. dissertation, Department of History of Science and Medicine, Yale University, 1972, University Microfilms Dissertation #73-14334; to be published as a monograph. It is worth pointing out that there exists a quite remarkable concentration of marble dials, including unfinished examples in the island of Delos, which seems to have been a sort of cult center and sundial factory of the ancient world. Because of this, one must consider that island as a good alternative candidate for the provenance of the Antikythera mechanism; neither it nor Rhodes would conflict with the archaeological evidence from the other objects.

antiquity that has come down to us relatively unharmed except for a gutted interior. It has never lost its roof nor been buried or demolished.[22] It stands, almost contemporaneous with the Antikythera fragments and indeed, closely associated with them in spirit and in scientific detail. We must say more of it later in connection with the historical tradition from which the Antikythera mechanism springs.

Though we know little of ancient science and technology directly from artifacts, there is always the evidence of the literature. Here, too, however, survival has been rather more selective than the long tradition of scholarship with rich sources leads us to suppose. It must not be forgotten that, for a text to survive, it usually has had to be such that it was worth the labor of hand-copying, re-editing, and probably also translating time after time as a classic until it could stretch through the ages and reach the relative sanctuary of the period of the printed book. Even quite important works by the most famous authors are known to us only through their listing by some biographer. And how many authors are known only by name, how many books by lesser authors have died quite unrecorded?

If this be true of the works that record the genius of great philosophers, the mathematicians, and the theoreticians of astronomy, it is doubly true of the record of technology. Even for much later periods before printing there are only the rarest accidental survivals of detailed sketches like those of the notebooks of Villard de Honnicourt (thirteenth century) and of Leonardo da Vinci (fifteenth century). From classical times there is almost nothing of this sort. What we have instead are a few books which describe the technical practices in civil and military engineering, architecture, and agriculture, and so on. In the first place these are often silent in just those places where we would wish for an exact statement of technical detail; in the second place we are dealing in all such works with what has become known as Low Technology, the sort of crafts that all men in all cultures have used in all ages for building homes and roads and water supply, making clothes and pots, growing and cooking food, waging war, etc. With the Antikythera mechanism, whatever its function, we are evidently concerned with the rather different phenomenon of High Technology. This is the name we give to those specially sophisticated crafts and manufactures that are in some ways intimately associated with the sciences, drawing on them for theories, giving to them the instruments and the techniques that enable men to observe and experiment and increase both knowledge and technical competence.

It is this High Technology that has provided the two chief traumatic historical changes that differentiated our present civilization from all that had gone before. In the middle of the seventeenth century, spreading out from chief centers in Florence, in London, and in Paris there came the Scientific Revolution which was founded partly upon changes in philosophical attitudes, partly on the newly widespread and powerful changes in the technology of communication by scientific journals which replaced individual correspondence, but partly, perhaps even principally, on the new availability of scientific instruments for experimentation. It has often been remarked that it is to the almost unknown but numerous group of mathematical practitioners that we should look to learn the reasons for the Scientific Revolution, rather than to the famous scientists of the period. The practitioners, the little men of science, were the instrument makers, the teachers of navigation and surveying, the writers of hack books on the useful scientific crafts. Through such men as their leader, Elias Allen, through the stronger and better organized colleagues in the Guild of Clockmakers, and through such contacts as Robert Hooke, the experimental operator of the Royal Society of London, they influenced the whole band of "amateurs of science" who constituted the first scientific societies. The amateurs were the customers of these practitioners, and every effort was made by the artisans to popularize and promote the use of mathematical and other scientific instruments.

Then again, beginning in the latter half of the eighteenth century, mostly in England, the movement known as the Industrial Revolution transformed the world once more, changing the entire pattern of world economics and producing a new sort of social force. The origin of this traumatic change also lay partly in the special crafts of high technology, particularly those of fine machine-making. In the textile industry and with the steam-pumping engines part of the craft derived from that of the wheelwright, the millwright, and the mining engineer. The dramatic changes, however, that made a revolution possible were most often those of ingenious new design based upon the craft of the instrument-maker and his close ally, the clockmaker. The textile machinery incorporated highly sophisticated linkwork and devices as complex as the differential gear, and it is no accident that James Watt first met the steam engine and was led to his great inventions by repairing a working lecture-demonstration model in his job as instrument-maker for a university.

As one traces back the roots of the Scientific and Industrial Revolutions beyond the fine machine-making and the scientific instruments, all the strands join together into a continuous thread of the great traditional craft of clockmaking. From the thirteenth century

---

[22] It has been analyzed by Joseph Noble and the present author in "The Water-Clock in the Tower of Winds," *Amer. Jour. Archaeology* **72**, 4 (October, 1968): pp. 345-355 and plates 111-118. See also my article "The Tower of Winds," *National Geographic Magazine* **131**, 4 (1967): pp. 586-596, illus. For the very interesting symbolism of the Tower see my paper, "The ✡, ☆, and ⚪, and other Geometrical and Scientific Symbolisms and Talismans," in: Mikulas Teich and Robert Young (eds.), *Changing Perspectives in the History of Science* (London, Heinemann, 1973).

onwards, after the European high Middle Ages had received the Islamic corpus of scientific learning, including that which had been transmitted from antiquity, this craft flourished. Beginning in the fifteenth century in the city states of Nuremberg and Augsburg the trade of the instrument-maker began to be specialized, but before and after this the clockmakers were also concerned with the design and making of all sorts of astrolabes, quadrants, sundials, and other scientific and astronomical instruments. The clockmakers were thus the prototypical group of practitioners and artisans who maintained in their technical traditions, and even in their guild structure as a profession, those special skills and qualities which were balanced between the sciences and the crafts and were to become the crucial element in giving the world the Scientific and Industrial Revolutions and the recent age of High Technology. The claim, of course, must not be pushed too far. The main line of clockmaking was, we may maintain, a necessary condition for this evolution, but it was by no means sufficient. As if to prove the claim one may expose on the dissecting board of history the case of Chinese civilization which had a very similar beginning but a quite different later stage. As Western clockmaking began, so did a tradition grow in the East, almost independently in classical and medieval times. By the time of the Scientific Revolution, however, the Eastern tradition lay broken, and development was begun again only by infusion from the West at the hands of the Jesuit missionaries.[23]

Thus, though not sufficient, the tradition of clockmaking can be seen to have been crucial to the emergence of our modern world. So much of present-day machinery derives from it that it has become commonplace to use the term "clockwork" for anything with gear wheels—as in clockwork toy trains for example. The timekeeping, ticking mechanical clock itself can be traced back only to the thirteenth or fourteenth century, but the wider history of clockwork goes back beyond the extraordinary emergence of the clock to a long prior period which includes the lines that lead also to such diverse developments as the concept of perpetual motion, the design of calculating machines and computers, to automata and robots, and to magnetic compasses.[24] It is in this story that the Antikythera mechanism provides us with dramatic new evidence and the earliest relic of such a distinguished main line in technology.

THE EARLY HISTORY OF GEARING AND CLOCKWORK

The historical origin of the toothed gear wheel is habitually misstated in the earlier specialized accounts and in most of the modern secondary treatments that rely on them.[25] The position has, however, now been clarified by the meticulous scholarship of A. G. Drachmann[26] with whose views I entirely agree. There are four different ways in which gear wheels were used to transmit motion or power; parallel wheels engaging each other, wheels at right angles engaging each other, a wheel engaging a toothed rack, and a wheel engaging an endless screw worm wheel. The first case in which parallel gears are meshed was formerly thought to be attested by a passage in the *Mechanical Problems* of Aristotle, which is generally attributed not to Aristotle himself but to the peripatic school, say 280 B.C. Drachmann has shown effectively that the passage in question is not decisive for there is no explicit mention of teeth on the wheels and they may just as well be smooth disk wheels in frictional contact. There is no other evidence in literature or in extant objects to indicate that this sort of gearing existed prior to the date of the Antikythera mechanism.

Evidence for the use of rack and pinion gearing at a similarly early date, *ca.* 280 B.C., is provided by Vitruvius (*ca.* 25 B.C.) who described it as a component in the water clock of Ktesibios. As Drachmann remarks, however, it seems to be a premature invention, for nothing like it is found in later water clocks where almost everything in the jackwork is moved by water power or by levers and strings. We are on more certain ground for the use of the gear turned by a worm wheel, for this is clearly invented by Archimedes, say about 250 B.C., and used in his war engines. Furthermore, the device is taken up by later inventors in other contexts. Heron (*ca.* 60 A.D.) uses it a great deal in his hodometer and dioptra, and gives a theory of it and details of its construction.

The earliest literary reference to gear wheels other than their use together with an Archimedean screw occurs in Vitruvius, *ca.* 25 B.C., where they are mentioned as a pair meshing at right angles in the construction of a water mill; this use later becomes quite common with the use of pegged wheels and lantern pinions. After this comes Heron who describes in his rather fanciful and probably impractical *barulkos* a method for using trains of gear wheels meshed in parallel fashion to raise a very heavy load with a very small effort.

---

[23] For this tradition see Joseph Needham, Wang Ling, and Derek de Solla Price, *Heavenly Clockwork* (Cambridge University Press, 1960).

[24] For a fuller account of this line see my monograph, "On the Origin of Clockwork, Perpetual Motion Devices, and the Compass," *Contributions from the Museum of History and Technology,* Smithsonian Institution Bulletin 218, No. 6 (1959): pp. 81–112.

[25] For monographic accounts of gear wheels the standard source has been Conrad Matschoss, *Geschichte des Zahnrades* (Berlin, Verein deutscher Ingenieure, 1940). A typical modern derivative is Darle W. Dudley, *The Evolution of the Gear Art* (Washington, D. C., American Gear Manufacturers Association, 1969).

[26] A. G. Drachmann, *The Mechanical Technology of Greek and Roman Antiquity* (Copenhagen, Munksgaard, 1963), especially pp. 200–203.

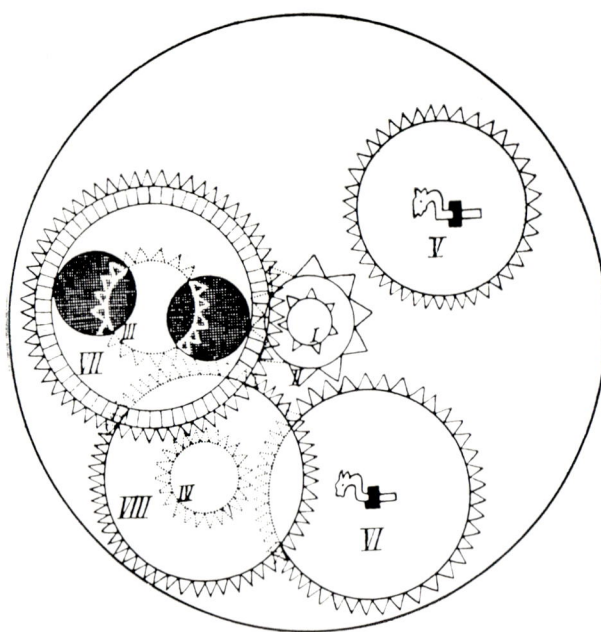

FIG. 41. Design by al-Biruni *ca.* 1000 A.D. for a geared solar and lunar calendar computer.

Thus although gear wheels are well attested from the time of Archimedes onwards, they occur only in combination with the rack in what may have been a one-shot invention ascribed by a much later source to Ktesibios, and in connection with Archimedes' own much used and surviving invention of the screw-worm wheel. Only a century later than that ascribed to the Antikythera mechanisms do we find evidence of the low technology use of a pair of gears to turn power through a right angle and the *barulkos* device which uses a very high gear ratio to move a heavy load and looks as if it came, as it probably does, from a schoolbook example of the function of parallel gears rather than from a practical mechanism.

Whatever the interpretation placed upon it, there is no question that the Antikythera mechanism has as its main features a very sophisticated train of many gears meshing in parallel planes and of widely assorted sizes; there is also the use of a contrate gear to turn the drive through a right angle in a very different style to that of the low technology millwright. Again, accepting even the widest possible limits for the dating of the inscription on the instrument and the archaeological evidence from the wreck, it is clear that we have something much more complicated than anything attested by the literary sources. On the other hand there is no actual conflict that would cause one to reject either the evidence from Antikythera or that from the literature. On the contrary, the detail of the gears from the mechanism follows faithfully that preserved in the illustrations of the Heronic and Vitruvian texts, especially in the feature that all gear teeth are exactly 60° equilateral triangles. Such teeth are relatively easy to shape by hand-sawing and filing—the technology of fine metal work, as evidenced from early Greek jewelry was capable of all the skills of fabrication many centuries before this.[27] It is worth noting that although such gear teeth are not very efficient for transmitting power —epicycloids being now preferred—they do function quite well in clockwork as evidenced from the operating de Dondi clock reconstructions now in the Science Museum, London, and the Museum of History and Technology, Washington (see fig. 44). The new evidence about Greek mechanisms forces some considerable re-evaluation of the old. We must suppose that from both Heron and Vitruvius we underestimate what was available in gearing technology in their times. It is a quite reasonable supposition since, after all, Vitruvius is writing a book on architecture, and Heron a book on theoretical mechanics and the basic elements of mechanism; neither of them represent their works as a treatment of all that could be done with complicated devices.

I believe that we have now evidence for the first time that Heron and Vitruvius are indeed on a side track from the main line of gearing, and that the true beginning is nearer to the clockwork of Ktesibios and what must have been a similar contribution by Archimedes himself. The mechanism from Antikythera represents a continuation of this main line either by a process of steady but unrecorded evolution or by a massive innovation by some unknown genius, contemporary with the similarly spectacular design of the Tower of Winds. Further we may safely suppose that this line continued and was transmitted to Islam, for we have both a text and a surviving instrument closely related to the Antikythera device and dating from *ca.* 1000 A.D. and 1221/22 A.D. (figs. 41, 42) respectively. These Islamic instruments in their turn bridge the gap by displaying considerable kinship both to the astrolabic water clocks of Islam and to the astronomical mechanical clocks of fourteenth-century Europe that founded the powerful and pervasive tradition of clockwork and thereby High Technology.

The evidence to support this conjecture comes, not from the history of the gear wheel, but from that of the planetarium. It is natural to take such a route when pursuing the historical ancestry of the mechanical clock in Europe because of the odd fact that the clock seems to come into being fully-fledged as a "fallen angel from the world of astronomy." The two earliest clocks we know are only very incidentally time-telling devices, and the crucial inventions of the escapement "tick-tock" and the weight drive are disregarded, left anonymous,

---

[27] In this respect see for example the very clear equilateral "gear tooth" decoration on the late fifth century B.C. Capitol Pin in the Museum of Fine Arts, Boston, published in H. Hoffman and T. F. Davidson, *Greek Gold* (Boston, etc., 1965), p. 187, fig. 70c. I am grateful to Professor C. S. Smith for calling my attention to this excellent example.

Fig. 42. Astrolabe containing geared calendar work. The instrument, now in the Museum for History of Science, Oxford, was made by M. b. Abi Bakr, Isfahan in 1221/2 A.D. and the gearing follows the design reported by al-Biruni *ca.* 1000 A.D. and contains many similar features to the Antikythera mechanism.

and not regarded by the authors as a matter of consequence. What was important was the enormously elaborate gear-work of the many dials to display all the motions of the stars and planets and the course of the calendar. In the clocks of Richard of Wallingford (*ca.* 1327–1330) and Giovanni de Dondi (1348–1364) we have such mechanisms described in detail [28] and one cannot doubt their ingenuity or the fact that they must have worked and been extremely impressive. So impressive were they in fact that the metaphor of the universe as a great clock became embodied in the philosophical and theological literature, and sketches of the mechanisms of the de Dondi clock account for two of the most complicated gearing diagrams in the sketchbooks of Leonardo da Vinci.[29]

I had previously thought that these early astronomical clocks were mechanizations of a prior tradition of non-mechanical but movable geometrical devices called equatoria that were used to calculate the positions of the planets from the Ptolemaic theory. Such devices seem to have been common during the Middle Ages and texts about them abound. In a sense it is still true that the early clocks were such mechanizations, but I think now that the tradition of the geared planetarium, moved by hand, or self-moving with the aid of a water clock, goes back to classical times.

Just like the history of gearing, that of the mechanized equatorium is based upon literary sources almost contemporary with the Antikythera mechanism, and they

[28] For the de Dondi clock see Silvio Bedini and Francis Maddison, "Mechanical Universe," *Trans. Amer. Philos. Soc.* **56**, 5 (Philadelphia, 1966). The Richard of Wallingford clock is subject of a forthcoming monographic book by Francis Maddison.

[29] Bedini and Maddison, *op. cit.*, p. 32.

FIG. 43. Interior mechanism of the Oxford astrolabe.

reach back to implicate Archimedes and perhaps also Ktesibios as the progenitors of the tradition. The prime authority is Cicero (b. 106, d. 43 B.C.) who went to study in Greece in 79 B.C. and settled in the island of Rhodes with Molon who had been one of his tutors, and with the stoic philosopher Posidonios of Apamea who Cicero says also made one of these Archimedean devices. Cicero returned to Rome in 77 B.C., which is just about the supposed time of the wreck of the Antikythera ship taking what must have been much the same route—but it would be asking too much of fortuitous circumstance to suppose that it is the baggage of the famous orator that now lies partly at the bottom of the sea and partly in the Greek National Archaeological Museum. At all events, Cicero did not lose his interest in Archimedes, for a little later, in 75 B.C. when he was *quaestor* in Sicily he identified the tomb of the mathematician from its geometrical diagram and restored it. I now give in full in translation the relevant texts from Cicero and the later writers. Cicero's descriptions of Archimedes' planetarium are:

For I remember an incident in the life of Gaius Sulpicius Gallus, a most learned man, as you know: at a time when a similar phenomenon was reported, and he happened to be at the house of Marcus Marcellus, his colleague in the consulship (166 B.C.), he ordered the celestial globe to be brought out which the grandfather of Marcellus had carried off from Syracuse, when that very rich and beautiful city was taken (212 B.C.), though he took home with him nothing else out of the great store of booty captured. Though I had heard this globe mentioned quite frequently on account of the fame of Archimedes, when I actually saw it I did not particularly admire it; for that other celestial globe, also constructed by Archimedes, which the same Marcellus placed in the temple of Virtue, is more beautiful as well as more widely known among the people. But when Gallus began to give a very learned explanation of the device, I concluded that the famous Sicilian had been endowed with greater genius than one would imagine it possible for a human being to possess. For Gallus told us that the other kind of celestial globe, which was solid and contained no hollow space, was a very early invention, the first one of that kind having been constructed by Thales of Miletus, and later marked by Eudoxus of Cnidus (a disciple of Plato, it was claimed) with the constellations and stars which are fixed in the sky. He also said that many years later Aratus, borrowing this whole arrangement and plan from Eudoxus, had described it in verse, without any knowledge of astronomy, but with considerable poetic talent. But this newer kind of globe, he said, on which were delineated the motions of the sun and moon and of those five stars which are called wanderers, or, as we might say, rovers, (i.e., the five planets) contained more than could be shown on the solid globe, and the invention of Archimedes deserved special admiration because he had thought out a way to represent accurately by a single device for turning the globe those various and divergent movements with their different rates of speed. And when Gallus moved the globe, it was actually true that the moon was always as many revolutions behind the sun on the bronze contrivance as would agree with the number of days it was behind it in the sky. Thus the same eclipse of the sun happened on the globe as it would actually happen, and the moon came to the point where the shadow of the earth was at the very time when the sun . . . out of the region. . . .

De re publica, I, xiv (21–22), Keyes's translation.

FIG. 44. Modern reconstruction from manuscript descriptions of the astronomical clock of Giovanni de Dondi, *ca.* 1364. Note the equilateral triangular teeth which survived in even later clockwork in spite of their inefficiency. Copyright Science Museum, London.

For when Archimedes fastened on a globe the movements of moon, sun and five wandering stars, he, just like Plato's God who built the world in the *Timaeus,* made one revolution of the sphere control several movements utterly unlike in slowness and speed. Now if in this world of ours phenomena cannot take place without the act of God, neither could Archimedes have reproduced the same movements upon a globe without divine genius.
Tusculan disputations, I 63, King's translation.

Later descriptions from Ovid (first century A.D.), Lactantius (fourth century A.D.), and Claudian (*ca.* 400 A.D.) respectively are:

This little spot, which now supports the Hall of Vesta, was then the great palace of unshorn Numa. Yet the shape of the temple, as it now exists, is said to have been its shape of old, and it is based on a sound reason. Vesta is the same as the Earth; under both of them is a perpetual fire; the earth and the hearth are symbols of the home. The earth is like a ball, resting on no prop; so great a weight hangs on the air beneath it. Its own power of rotation keeps its orb balanced; it has no angle which could press on any part; and since it is placed in the middle of the world and touches no side more or less, if it were not convex, it would be nearer to some part than to another, and the universe would not have the earth as its central weight. There stands a globe hung by Syracusan art in closed air, a small image of the vast vault of heaven, and the earth is equally distant from the top and bottom. That is brought about by its round shape. The form of the temple is similar: there is no projecting angle in it; a dome protects it from the showers of rain.
Ovid, *Fasti,* VI, 263–283, Frazer's translation.

Could Archimedes the Sicilian have devised from hollow brass a likeness and figure of the world, in which he so arranged the sun and moon that they should effect unequal motions and those like to the celestial changes for each day, as it were, and display or exhibit, not only the risings and settings of the sun and the waxings and wanings of the moon, but even the unequal courses of revolutions and the wanderings of the stars as that sphere turned, and yet God Himself be unable to fashion and accomplish what the skill of a man could simulate by imitation? Which answers, therefore, would a Stoic give if he had seen the forms of stars painted and reproduced in that sphere? Would he say that they were moved by their own purpose or would he not rather say by the skill of the designer?
Lactantius, *The Divine Institutes,* II, 5, 18, McDonald's translation.

Archimedes' sphere. When Jove looked down and saw the heavens figured in a sphere of glass he laughed and said to the other gods: "Has the power of mortal effort gone so far? Is my handiwork now mimicked in a fragile globe? An old man of Syracuse has imitated on earth the laws of the heavens, the order of nature, and the ordinances of the gods. Some hidden influence within the sphere directs the various courses of the stars and actuates the lifelike mass with definite motions. A false zodiac runs through a year of its own, and a toy moon waxes and wanes month by month. Now bold invention rejoices to make its own heaven revolve and sets the stars in motion by human wit. Why should I take umbrage at harmless Salmoneus and his mock thunder? Here the feeble hand of man has proved Nature's rival."
Claudian, *Shorter Poems* (*ca.* A.D. 400), Number LI (LXVIII), Platnauer's translation.

A similar arrangement seems to be indicated in another mechanized globe, also mentioned by Cicero and said to have been made by Posidonius of Rhodes:

When you see a statue or a painting, you recognize the exercise of art; when you observe from a distance the course of a ship, you do not hesitate to assume that its motion is guided by reason and by art; when you look at a sun-dial or a water-clock, you infer that it tells the time by art and not by chance how then can it be consistent to suppose that the world, which includes both the works of art in question, the craftsmen who made them, and everything else besides, can be devoid of purpose and of reason? Suppose a traveller to carry into Scythia or Britain the orrery recently constructed by our friend Posidonius, which at each revolution reproduces the same motions of the sun, the moon and the five planets that take place in the heavens every day and night, would any single native doubt that this orrery was the work of a rational being? These thinkers however raise doubts about the world itself from which all things arise and have their being, and debate whether it is the product of chance or necessity of some sort, or of divine reason and intelligence; they think more highly of the achievement of Archimedes in making a model of the revolutions of the firmament than of that of nature in creating them, although the perfection of the original shows a craftsmanship many times as great as does the counterfeit.
De natura deorum, II, xxxiv–xxxv (87–88), Rackham's translation.

In spite of a tantalizing lack of technical details it is clear that Cicero was stimulated by activity in the construction of these mechanical "spheres" in the school of Posidonius when he was at Rhodes in 79–77 B.C. and that there was at this time some first-hand knowledge of at least two such devices made by Archimedes which survived as booty taken from Syracuse to Rome, one in the house of the Marcellus family and another in the Temple of Virtue. The essence of the mechanism which has been added to the older static globe of fixed stars is a new mechanical device which shows the rotation in the zodiac of the Sun and the Moon, the classical five planets, and the phases and perhaps also eclipses for the Moon. It is perhaps worth pointing out that what seems to impress Cicero most is that the mechanism takes the (sidereal) motions of the Sun and the Moon and produces from them the correct (synodic) waxing and waning of the Moon's phases, for this is the feature to which the greater part of the surviving mechanism from the Antikythera fragments is devoted.

If we are to credit Archimedes for even the simplest possible device of the sort mentioned we must assume that he used a set of gears meshing in parallel planes to give the correct mean periodic rotations to the seven celestial bodies and the synodic month. No other mechanism of strings and pulleys or anything else would give so appropriately the behavior of the interlocking regular cycles that constituted the main corpus of astronomical theory at the time of Archimedes. Gears fitting together could reproduce faithfully the traditional values for the mean periods of the planets. Thus a 30/1 gear ratio would be used to carry a pointer indicating the place of the planet Saturn which moves round the zodiac once in a period of 30 years during which the Sun has made 30 revolutions. Similar arrangements would be made for the 12-year mean period of Jupiter and probably a 2½-year period for Mars. If this is reasonable for representing planetary motions, it is much more forcibly suggested by the relentlessly even, day-by-day, month-by-month, year-by-year progress of the calendrical cycles involving the Sun and the Moon. The cycles of Meton and Euctemon (fl. *ca.* 430 B.C.) and Calippus (late fourth century B.C.) are such that gearing will provide a beautiful and elegant demonstration to impress any student of them. A wheel of 19 teeth engaging with one of 235 teeth will as they turn together show tooth by tooth the way in which the cycle of the years is enmeshed with that of the synodic months. If one attempts to add more wheels to give the cycles of the days or of the siderial months, one gets exactly the sort of device referred to by Cicero, preserved in the Antikythera fragments, and continued in the Islamic and later European geared devices.

In a device of this sort, complications will arise quite naturally both from the astronomical necessity and from the number-theoretic relations of the desired gear ratios. For example with the 235/19 ratio mentioned above, though one may wish to use gear wheels having numbers of teeth that are easy to mark out by geometrical construction, this is not possible. The numerator has prime factors of 5 and 47, and the denominator is already a prime, so that the ratio can be achieved only by some such gear train [30] as for example $60 - 12 + 47 - 19$ where there will always remain wheels having the awkward numbers of 19 and 47 teeth or some multiple thereof. From astronomical necessity undoubtedly the most telling is the relation between the siderial motions of the Sun and Moon and the Moon's synodic cycle of phases; exactly that which impressed Cicero. For the Metonic cycle, for example, of 19 years and 235 synodic months, it is absolutely necessary that the Moon make $235 + 19 = 254$ siderial revolutions in the complete cycle, since theoretically the synodic month is produced by the rate at which the Moon outruns the Sun in its passage round the zodiac. Either one can simply build such a consistent set of numbers into the system, for example by adding a ratio of 254/19 to that which gives the basic cycle, or one can take the elegant but mechanically difficult route of providing a mechanism that starts with two of the rotation rates and generates the third by mechanical summing and differencing. This latter route seems to have been that which motivated the inclusion of a differential gear turntable in the Antikythera mechanism.

Since the astronomical cycles are such a natural target for gear-work, leading on to step-by-step increases in complication, and since we now have the evidence of the Antikythera mechanism to support the remarks made by Cicero and later writers about the planetarium of Archimedes, I think we may safely re-interpret the historical position. Archimedes evidently must have taken the first steps to mechanize the mean motions of the Sun and Moon and planets and incorporated this mechanism into elegant and impressive devices which survived in Rome for many years. He may also have made an exception to his custom of not committing to writing his ingenious inventions, for among his lost works is listed a treatise, "On Sphere-making," which may well have given this semi-mathematical material of the planetarium rather than a simple description of the marking of stars on a ball. In this planetarium Archimedes would have used, perhaps for the first time, sets of gears arranged to mesh in parallel planes, and he would have been led to the rather elegant number manipulation which is necessary to get a set of correct ratios for turning the various planetary markers.

He may also have used his favorite worm-wheel construction to turn the gear-train system one tooth at a time in order to achieve the large ratio necessary for showing the daily rotation in addition to those of the Sun and Moon and planets. Perhaps it should also be remarked that there appears in the literature a text on the "Clock of Archimedes." It is preserved in Arabic manuscripts which ascribe the origin of the work not only to Archimedes but to Heron and Philon also.[31] The design of the monumental piece is similar to the other Islamic clocks of Ridwan and al-Jazari. The clepsydra has a variable depth hole to make it follow the seasonal hours, and the sinking float works a pair of linear scales and makes the eyes move on a central face. It also is geared through a contrate wheel to a device to make a bird spit a ball into a gong basin every hour on the hour, and the outflow water from the clepsydra is used for a typical Heronic singing-bird display below. Though the clock is obviously in the great tradition that runs from Ktesibios to Philon, there is no way of knowing the point or points of the sequence from which it springs, nor even of distinguishing any part that is Hellenistic from that which may be later Islamic elaboration. In particular there is nothing of the astronomical clockwork tradition here, only the later Heronic automaton display technique, and it is suggested therefore that the name of Archimedes is invoked only as the founder, or co-founder with Ktesibios, of the automated water-clock tradition. Perhaps some day a deeper study of the Islamic tradition may sort out these Hellenistic elements contained in it, and throw more

---

[30] We use here the standard notation for describing a gear train. The numbers give the tooth count of each wheel. Two numbers linked by a dash (—) represent gears that mesh together. Two numbers linked by a plus (+) represent gears on the same shaft turning together.

[31] Edited by Eilhard Wiedemann and Fritz Hauser, "Über eine dem Archimedes zugeschriebene Uhr," *Nova Acta Academiae Caesareae Leopoldina-Carolinae Germanicae Naturae Curiosorum* **103**, 2 (Halle, 1918): pp. 164-202.

light on the work of Archimedes and the other mechanical innovators.

Cicero does not mention any intervening authorities on the making of such planetarium spheres, so we may reasonably suppose that the Archimedean tradition was taken up again only in the period in which he found it flourishing in the school of Posidonios in Rhodes in 78 B.C. Though there may not have been significant development in either gearing or in planetarium construction between Archimedes and Posidonios there had been a very great change in astronomical theory and in instrument-making due to two advances made by Hipparchus, who flourished probably also in Rhodes ca. 162–126 B.C. One effect of the work of Hipparchus was to make planetary theory considerably more complicated geometrically than the matter of simple rotational cycles which it had been in the earliest phase. A second change due to Hipparchus came about through his introduction of the stereographic projection which enables one to map a sphere on a flat surface in such a way that problems such as those of spherical astronomy can be solved easily by plane geometry and trigonometry.

The force of the first change was that it rendered unsatisfactory the sort of representation that could easily be obtained for planetary motions by means of simple gearing. I believe that it might well have made the planetary geared model virtually unobtainable in practice from that time until the highly elaborate constructions of Richard of Wallingford and Giovanni de Dondi restored the Archimedean intentions in the later Middle Ages. At any rate we have no records and not even literary evidence for any mechanized planetary models after Archimedes except for that of Posidonios who may well have preserved the simple original system. The force of the second change was to enable the makers of models to avoid the cumbersome and inconvenient use of a globe and enable them to represent the universe on flat plates and dials. It seems likely that the first use was in the anaphoric clock in which a disk is marked out as a star map using the stereographic projection and rotated by a water clock behind a spider-web *arachne* of circular arcs which map the horizon and several lines of equal altitude and equal azimuth for the place in question.[32] If the plate is fitted with a representation of the ecliptic with holes so that a Sun and perhaps a Moon can be plugged in at positions appropriate to the day of observation, the turning disk will show the risings and settings of Sun, Moon and fixed stars, and by the passage of the Sun past the lines of the *arachne* it will indicate the hours of the day and of the night. Thus such a device gives a very impressive representation of all the features of the diurnal rotation of the heavens.

First, the anaphoric clock was used to replace the indicators which Ktesibios had worked by a rack and pinion in his water clock and substituted for the special device controlling water flow at rates appropriate to the seasons. As such it was described by Vitruvius, and exactly such a device seems to have been the central feature inside the Tower of Winds. A fragment from such an anaphoric clock disk, inscribed in Roman letters and dating apparently from the second century A.D. has been found at Salzburg. Secondly, the principle of the anaphoric clock seems to have been reversed for convenience; the fragile *arachne* being replaced by a solid disk inscribed with the network of arcs of circles, and the turning portion becoming an open-work pierced plate containing pointers marking the position of the dozen or so brightest stars and a circle marked with the zodiacal signs and the ecliptic. In this form it is the astrolabe, the most important scientific instrument of the Islamic and European Middle Ages, extending into the Renaissance with perhaps a thousand examples known, dating from the ninth century onwards. Byzantine, Syriac, and Islamic texts have been preserved but it seems likely that this instrument too must have originated in the Greco-Roman period and it is even faintly possible that it could be another product of the Rhodian school of Posidonios.

Under these modifications the exhibition of the astronomical universe became changed from what it had been for Archimedes. The solid sphere was replaced by an anaphoric clock representation as in the Tower of Winds, and the emphasis was taken away from the five planets which were either shown in simplified form or marked on a dial where the anomalies in their motions could be taken care of by appropriate inscriptions rather than by epicyclic gear assemblies. The emphasis thus was moved to a display of the geared cycles of the Sun and Moon and the resultant synodic month, and perhaps also some mechanization of the eclipse cycle or the motion of the Moon's nodes. I think also that there could have been added at this time another transition from solid to flat model, a representation of the phase of the Moon, not by a painted ball, but by a marked disk painted part black, part white, and viewed through a little window. Such a device occurs in the geared device by al-Biruni and in the geared astrolabe founded upon this text; it is a device still to be found in the dials of recent grandfather clocks, and as a separate Moon-phase instrument or in combination with sundials it is very common in medieval texts and in the work of Renaissance instrument-makers. At all events, as a result of the Hipparchan modifications the Archimedean planetarium evolved most probably into just the sort of Sun and Moon cycle calculator device that seems attested from the Antikythera fragments and from the later history of clockwork astronomical models.

Since we do not know for certain whether the Antikythera mechanism was driven automatically by water power or turned by hand, it is perhaps unfair to call it

---

[32] Here I have followed the very convincing arguments of A. G. Drachmann, "The Plane Astrolabe and Anaphoric Clock," *Centaurus* 3 (1954): pp. 183–189, and O. Neugebauer, "The Early History of the Astrolabe," *Isis* 40 (1949): pp. 240–256.

a "calculator." If automatic it is more properly an exhibition device, an elaborate clock-dial assembly; if manual it is still primarily an elegant demonstration or simulation of the heavens, more like an astrolabe perhaps than a direct ancestor of the calculating machines of Pascal and Leibniz. Nevertheless, it does use fixed gear ratios to make these calculations of the soli-lunar calendar and it does this more by using pointer readings on a digital dial than by causing a direct geometrical modeling of the paths of the planets in space. The mechanism displays the cyclical sequence of sets of discrete phenomena rather than a continuum of events in a flowing time. In this way it is perhaps more in the spirit of Babylonian astronomy and the modern digital computer than in that of Greek geometrical models and the automated sphere of Archimedes.

Finally it must be added that another big change also occurred in this period. It is nowhere in evidence from the Antikythera mechanism, though it may have been involved in the Tower of Winds, and it left a considerable legacy to the great clocks of the Islamic and European Middle Ages. The simulation of the heavens had only been one-half of the tradition of glorifying man's comprehension of creation by acting as Gods, making their own universes. The astronomical half was complemented by a series of devices that limited living beings, automata in the forms of birds that flapped their wings and whistled, mannikins that gyrated, moved their heads, and blew trumpets and banged gongs and drums. The simulation was not entirely trivial. Just as in the astronomical automata nobody seriously believed that the perfect working of the planetarium proved that the stars and planets were really turned by clockwork, so nobody thought that the strings and pulleys, water pipes and pneumatic contrivances duplicated the workings of biology. Nevertheless, these models played a considerable role in developing what was essentially a mechanistic philosophy in which the workings of human and animal physiology could reasonably be ascribed to humors and fluids coursing through the tubes of the body and muscles that moved like ropes.

Such simulated figures are given most adequate treatment in the *Automaton Theater* of Heron where the display is often most elegant and complicated though the mechanical principles used are ingenious combinations of strings and levers and pulleys. Nowhere does Heron use gears in this work. Indeed the historians of technology have often complained with some pique that the most complex technological texts from antiquity concern nothing more than these "toys" instead of useful working machinery. The point has been missed that these automata were in fact combined with the astronomical models to produce displays of both halves of creation together, and this is why they appear as such not only through Byzantium, Islam, and the European Middle Ages but right down to the modern Black Forest cuckoo clock. If this also seems comparatively trivial it should be remembered also that, in addition to the contribution to conceptual model-making in early physiology, such models were the source from which all of our powerful modern tradition of automation springs. The legacy of these early robots is far from trivial, and along the way the "toys" were a carrier, as were the astronomical clockworks, for a large share of man's most sophisticated fine mechanical technologies.

THE INVENTION OF COMPLICATED CLOCK-WORK AND THE DIFFERENTIAL GEAR

Even though the differential gear may have made its appearance in the Antikythera mechanism through the motivation to exhibit the motions of the Sun and Moon in perfect consistency with the phases of the Moon, it is nevertheless surprising to find such a sophisticated device so early. In my experience it is difficult even today to explain the theory of this gear-work to the bulk of people in a modern audience familiar with a host of mechanical and electronic devices. It must surely rank as one of the greatest basic mechanical inventions of all time, and whether the inventor was Archimedes himself or some unknown ingenious mechanic of the school of Posidonios he should be accorded the highest honors. It should by the way be noted that in spite of assertions in several secondary works the differential gear occurs nowhere in the works of Leonardo da Vinci and is not used in the de Dondi clock. The differential gear [33] does not appear again until it occurs in a complicated globe clock made by Eberhart Baldewin, the predecessor of the famous clockmaker Jobst Bürgi (the Second Archimedes, as he was called) at the Court of Landgraf Wilhelm IV at Kassel in 1575. The clock, which is now in the Ilbert Collection at the British Museum, uses a differential gear with contrate pinions on a disk driven by a worm wheel to convert the 365 turns of solar day axle into 366 turns which are needed for the proper siderial day revolution of the star globe. Similar differential gears can be found in many astronomical clocks of the sixteenth and seventeenth cen-

---

[33] For the history of the differential gear, see H. von Bertele, "The Origin of the Differential Gear and its Connection with Equation Clocks," *Trans. Newcomen Soc.* 30 (London, 1955/56/57): pp. 145–155. For the Baldewin clock I have used H. Alan Lloyd, *Some Outstanding Clocks over Seven Hundred Years* (London, Leonard Hill Books Limited, 1958): pp. 57–60. I have given here no mention of the differential gearing alleged to have been included in the South-Pointing Chariots built in China by the engineers Yen Su and Wu Tê-Jen in the years 1027 and 1107. A full account of the obviously complex mechanisms and the several ingenious reconstructions thereof has been given by Joseph Needham, *Science and Civilisation in China* 4, 2 (Cambridge University Press, Cambridge, 1965): pp. 286–303, but I do not feel convinced that the texts will bear a differential gear interpretation, and even if they did it would seem likely to be a strand of historical development quite independent of the Western line here described.

turies where it is commonly used, as in the Antikythera mechanism, to mediate between the synodic and siderial months. Later it is also used to bring into the clock a cam motion for the Equation of Time and for Tidal Dials. One must assume that the principle was common knowledge not long after 1575 and that it was introduced in the same astronomical clockwork context in which it seems to have started.

Several times in the eighteenth century there appear to have been more or less independent reinventions of the principle of the differential gear in clockwork, notably by Joseph Williamson in 1719–1725, by Dauthiau who claimed in 1765 to have invented it some fifteen years earlier, and by the brothers Aureliano and David a San Cajetano who studied it intensively and built clocks as well as producing a theoretical study of the kinematics of differential gearing in 1793. Early in the nineteenth century, by which time the basic principle of the device may have become common knowledge among mechanicians outside the craft of the clockmaker, the differential gear makes its first appearance in the textile industry. Almost simultaneously, perhaps both making independent inventions, perhaps one learning from the other, perhaps both deriving from the clockmaker tradition, it is the subject of patents by Asa Arnold of Rhode Island in 1823, and by Henry Houldsworth and a tinsmith called Green in England in the same year.

The gear was used in both cases in the bobbin-and-fly frame for cotton manufacture, being applied to the roving so as to regulate the variable velocity which was required for winding the fine filaments of cotton evenly on the bobbin. It was this that enabled cotton yarn to be mass-produced at greater rate and lower cost while improving the quality of the product, and as such it revolutionized one of the most economically important industries of the period. From the textile mills the differential gear migrated into the automobile by a route which happens to be traceable. The person involved was Richard Roberts who had started as a worker on textile machinery in the 1840's and had learned machine-shop practice with Maudsley; it was he who first designed a steam road vehicle which used the differential gear in order to make the powered wheels steerable—the same purpose for which it is still applied in the modern automobile from which it is now most generally familiar to mechanics.

There is, therefore, a reasonably direct route from the use of differential gearing in Renaissance clocks to the present day, but one can say nothing as to the question of whether the Renaissance use was a direct transmission from the old tradition of astronomical clockwork or whether it was a reinvention by another brilliant mechanic in the same stimulating context. Whether it be invention or reinvention, the basic question remains; what leads to the appearance of such sophisticated devices so early in the tradition? Part of the answer lies, I think, in the fact that in any case the tradition of gearing was already quite far advanced by the time the differential gear makes its appearance. Even if the interval is only that from Archimedes to the time of Cicero, there would have been about 150 years to breed a familiarity. The other part of the answer is closely associated with the problem of why the earliest medieval clocks, and perhaps the earliest of those in the Renaissance tradition too, happen to be so much more complicated than those that come later.

Perhaps there is a particular sort of inventive mind that has its particular brilliance in the perception of such things as the complex relationship of a gear system or an involved mechanism. I suggest that Archimedes, and the anonymous master of the school of Posidonios, and Richard of Wallingford, Giovanni de Dondi, Eberhard Baldewin, Jobst Bürgi were all innovative mechanical geniuses of this sort. It must be very rare that such genius is combined with another that leads to the other things for which men become famous, but such is true for Archimedes and indeed for Leonardo da Vinci who would almost certainly have been unsung if they had been only mechanicians. The people with this sort of mind may not be nearly as uncommon as their lack of notoriety would lead us to suppose. I suggest that it is probably the same trait of mechanical ingeniousness that one finds in thousands of proud but unknown nineteenth-century patent-holders, many great experimentalists and engineers whose skills became obvious even in childhood when they were entranced by the creations possible with a toy erector or meccano set, and perhaps also in the new generation of young geniuses whose perception is now transferred from gearwheels to computer programs.

I think that several times in history such genius has made geared astronomical clockwork so far ahead of his time that after him the development has rested for awhile to emerge with a tradition augmented more by stimulus diffusion than by direct continuation of the idea. A technological tradition is something so much more fragile than anything that was encoded into a written book and transmitted into the orderly fashion of knowledge. Each advance filtering down led to a debasement of the original brilliance, but the technological availability led, after some gap in time, to application for more and more socially useful results.

For the Antikythera mechanism, I think it is necessary to assume the existence of a genius of this customary sort, and it seems more likely to be an anonymous mechanician of Rhodes, rather than that of Archimedes who would otherwise have to be credited not merely with the invention of fine mechanical gearing of all sorts and with its application to astronomical clockwork, but also with the next huge stage of conceiving the differential gear. We know of no such mechanician, but they were most often poorly recorded even in more recent times, and in any case the historical and the archaeological record for Rhodes is so much poorer than many other important centers of Greco-Roman science and technology.

Even so we know of many likely candidates for the authorship of the Antikythera mechanism including Andronicus Kyrrhestes who built the Tower of Winds and also one of the most complicated astronomical sundials on the island of Tenos, Posidonios himself, whose work in this area is attested by the statement of Cicero, Geminos, whose luni-solar cycle theory and parapegma calendar of the *Isagoge* is the closest text we have to the inscriptions on the mechanism, and perhaps others of this period. We know also from the island of Rhodes a somewhat mysterious and fragmentary inscription which was excavated in Keskinto near Lindos and appears to contain the numberical parameters for a complete planetary system. In all it seems that in Rhodes of the period, though there may have been no astronomers or mathematicians of the greatest genius there were all the conditions and interests for a mechanic of genius to follow in the tradition of Archimedes and build the mechanism that was retrieved from the Antikythera wreck.

APPENDIX

I. COMPOSITION OF THE METAL FRAGMENTS

The chemical composition of the Antikythera fragments appears to have been investigated by Damberge in the course of studies connected with the cleaning of the bronze statues from the wreck. His analysis does not seem to have been published in full, though Rediadis cited the central result in 1910. From this it would seem that the metal was a simple bronze containing about 4.1 per cent of tin alloyed with the main component of copper.

To confirm and extend this result I asked permission from the authorities of the National Archaeological Museum for small quantities of the crumbled debris from the fragments to be removed for study. This was graciously granted by Dr. Karouzos, and similar small samples were transmitted to Professor Earle R. Caley of the Ohio State University for chemical analysis and to Professor Cyril Stanley Smith then at the Institute for the Study of Metals, University of Chicago (now at the Massachusetts Institute of Technology) for metallurgical and spectroscopic study. I am most grateful to them and to their assistants for their careful and valuable work. Their reports are appended. In brief, they confirm that the metal was a bronze, no other metals being present as more than the expected impurities. In particular, the bronze, unlike the later Greek bronzes, contained no large amount of lead, and it does not seem to have been originally gilded. The bronze had been worked by cold hammering and then annealed at a dull red heat, presumably in the course of preparation of the fairly uniform metal sheet out of which almost all the preserved portions seem to have been fabricated by sawing and filing and drilling. The small amount of lead may well be due to the presence of soldered joints—at least one occurs at a place where a gear tooth has been mended by the inset of a soldered plate (see p. 35), and the presence of a trace of iron in one sample but not in the other may be due to the presence of a small pin of that metal used in some slot-and-wedge joint.

Caley's suggestion that the sheet may be earlier in date than the machine is particularly interesting, though of course we do not have anything like an ample series of analyses of Greek bronzes. Even if we had, there would be much difficulty in asserting that all lead-free bronze objects must be earlier than those containing much lead. If, however, Caley is right in this, one would presumably suppose that the sheet metal used in the instrument had been cut from a large uniform plate—it would have to be at least three square feet in area—made in more ancient times. An old plate carrying an inscription would have served very well. Unfortunately, there seems to be no trace of any old inscriptions on the undersides of the preserved plates.

REPORT OF PROFESSOR EARLE R. CALEY

A sample of the corrosion products was examined for the purpose of establishing the identity of the metal used in the construction of the mechanism. This sample, which was composed of small particles of corrosion products from the object, was supplied by the Director of the National Museum of Athens. These particles had the form of flat fragments, irregular grains, and coarse powder. Most of them were dark or light green in color, some were dark or light gray, and a few were black. No free metal could be detected among or within any of the particles. The total weight of this very heterogeneous sample amounted to only a few centigrams. Because it did not appear to be truly representative of the corrosion products as a whole, and because its weight was so small, no quantitative analysis of the sample was attempted. The results here reported were obtained from a systematic qualitative chemical analysis on a semi-micro scale, and from supplementary separate tests.

Copper, in the form of various compounds, was found to be the metallic element present in largest proportion. Tin was found to be present in much smaller proportion, apparently in the form of stannic oxide. Iron, which was probably present in the form of ferric oxide or hydrated ferric oxide, was the only other metallic element that was detected. The proportion of iron appeared to be smaller than that of the tin. Gold, silver, lead, nickel, and zinc were sought but none of these was detected. Since the absence of lead seemed to be of special interest, this fact was confirmed by different independent tests. Carbon, chlorine, and sulfur were present as carbonate, chloride, and sulfide, respectively. Most, and perhaps all of these, were combined with the copper. Silicon was present in small proportion in the form of silica, and possibly also in the form of silicate. Of course, oxygen was present in the form of oxides and other compounds, though no tests were actually made for this element.

The results of this examination indicate that the unaltered metal of the mechanism was a simple tin bronze. Whether this was a normal bronze, or one that contained an unusually low or unusually high proportion of tin, could not be determined from these qualitative results. That the proportion of tin could have been determined by a quantitative analysis seems doubtful in view of the possibility that the ratio of copper to tin in the corrosion products might have been very different from that in the unaltered metal. The absence of lead compounds among the corrosion products is surprising since lead is a normal component of ancient bronzes. Though lead is often present in very low proportion as an impurity in early Greek bronzes, it is usually present as a principal component in those of late date, and in those made as late as the first century B.C. the proportion of lead often exceeds that of the tin. It is not unlikely that lead compounds would be absent from the corrosion products of a bronze that contained lead as a mere impurity, or that they would be present in such small proportion as to escape detection, but it is very unlikely that they would be absent from the corrosion products of a bronze that contained a moderate or high proportion of lead. Even if the small random sample supplied for this examination was poorly representative of the corrosion products in a quantitative sense, it seems unlikely that lead compounds would have been entirely absent even for this sample had the unaltered metal contained lead as a principal component. The results of this examination therefore suggest that the bronze used in the construction of the mechanism may have been manufactured much earlier than the first century B.C.

REPORT OF PROFESSOR CYRIL S. SMITH

There was an inadequate amount of material for a chemical analysis, but it was examined spectrographically. Two samples were studied, one an average sample of the miscellaneous debris, the other selected compact particles from the core of the original sheet (see below).

The results of the spectrochemical analysis are summarized in table 5. The material was bronze of good quality. It would be reasonable to suppose that the tin content was about 5 per cent, which agrees with its microstructure. There is no trace of zinc; hence the suggestion that the mechanism was made of brass is completely negated. The iron, antimony, and arsenic

TABLE 5

SPECTROGRAPHIC ANALYSIS OF DEBRIS FROM ANTIKYTHERA MECHANISM

Element	Average sample	Selected fragments
Copper	Main constituent	Main constituent
Tin	1–10%	1–10%
Lead	0.3	0.6
Arsenic	0.1	0.1
Sodium	0.1	0.1
Nickel	0.06	0.1
Gold	0.06	0.04
Iron	0.05	0.05
Antimony	0.02	0.04
Bismuth	0.02	0.04

In addition to the significant components listed above, both samples contained about 0.01 per cent of aluminum, molybdenum, calcium, and cobalt; about 0.001 to 0.005 per cent of magnesium, vanadium, silver, boron and chromium. Zinc and mercury were undetected (i.e., less than about 0.02 per cent). No other elements were found.

The figures are based on a visual estimate of relative line intensities and are only approximations. There could be an error by as much as ±50 per cent of the values given. The spectrographic analyses were done on ten milligram samples, burned to completion in a 10 amp. DC arc and photographed in the wave length range 2250 to 4800 angstroms.

contents, though significant, are undoubtedly normal impurities. The gold content is not unusual for an ancient copper alloy. It is just possible that the sheet had been gilded, although no trace of gold could be observed under the microscope, and it is therefore concluded that the gold that is present was an unintentional impurity in the metal itself. The sodium, calcium, and aluminum were probably merely absorbed from the sea water, and the other elements, all of which are in insignificant amounts, are natural impurities.

MICROSTRUCTURE

There were two flat bits, roughly a millimeter across, which were compact enough for metallographic ex-

(a)

FIG. 45. Metallurgical microphotographs of a sample of metal from the Antikythera mechanism. (a) times 75; (b) times 250; (c) times 500.

(b)

(c)

amination. These were found to consist principally of corrosion product, though with some residual uncorroded metal. The larger of these fragments was about 0.6 millimeter thick, which is supposedly about the thickness of the original sheet. The fragment was composed of three layers, the two outer ones being composed of a soft corrosion product 0.07 to 0.12 millimeter thick, which had become detached except locally (fig. 45a). This layer was entirely missing from the other fragment. The inner part, 0.33 to 0.42 millimeter thick, was partly metallic, with compact corrosion product, as shown in figures 45 b, c, at magnifications of 250 and 500 respectively. This corrosion product had been formed in a manner definitely related to the microstructure of the metal. Attack had obviously proceeded first along the grain boundaries and then in a definite crystallographic form within the grains themselves, which is revealed by the geometric criss-cross patterns observable in the photomicrograph. The angles between the lines of corrosion product were measured in twelve grains, and in every case the angular relationships confirmed the belief that they correspond to the (111) planes (octahedral planes) in the cubic system. Sometimes they lay along the boundaries of the annealing twins. This configuration of corrosion product is not observed in ordinary rapid corrosion of copper-base alloys, although it has been seen in a number of other ancient bronzes. It is Case III in the paper "Microscopic Study of Ancient Bronze and Copper" by C. G. Fink and E. P. Poluskin (*Trans. Amer. Inst. Mechanical Engineers* **122** (1936): pp. 90–120) and is not observed in castings or in worked bronzes that have been fully annealed, but it follows the slip planes produced by cold deformation. Though slip bands were not visible in the uncorroded parts of the metal after etching, and the grain structure of the whole was not perceptibly distorted, the metal had probably been slightly cold-worked, for example, in a final planishing operation or by the tracing tool used to apply the inscriptions or graduations.

The corrosion product at the surfaces of the one piece (and which had supposedly become detached from the other and lost) is mineralogically distinct from the corrosion product in the core in direct contact with the metal and is much softer. It is perhaps an oxychloride which is formed by further mineralization *in situ* of the primary corrosion products. There was no change in the gross arrangement during this conversion, and the original grain boundaries and the geometric markings of the first stage of the corrosion are clearly preserved. There are probably two different minerals involved, tin-rich and copper-rich respectively, though we have not identified either.

There are a few large gray inclusions of slag in the original metal, which are preserved and become even more clearly visible in the corroded layer. These inclusions undoubtedly originated in the casting operation and became somewhat elongated during the working of the metal into the form of sheet. In general, the microstructure is that of an annealed bronze consisting of the alpha solid-solution phase alone. There is no trace of the second phase, beta (or its composition products), which appears in structural equilibrium above about 14 per cent tin but at lower concentrations in castings that have not been annealed. The average grain size of the alpha phase is about 0.02 mm. The microhardness measured in the uncorroded areas of five different grains varied between 38 and 62 kg/mm^2 (Vickers diamond test 2 gram load). These low values suggest an annealed bronze containing less than 5 per cent tin.

This examination shows that the original metal had been worked fairly extensively, probably by cold hammering with intermediate anneals and then finally annealed at about 500–600° Centigrade (a dull red heat). The grains are uniform in size and shape, which precludes crude hot hammering—in any event a bronze of this composition is not easy to work when hot—and indicates fairly extensive and uniform cold working prior to the final annealing, which must have been the last metallurgical operation.

The spectrographic analysis was done by Miss Myrtle Bachelder, and the micrographs were made by Mmes. Betty Neilson and Stanka Jovanovic, all of the staff of the Institute for the Study of Metals, University of Chicago, March, 1959.

II. TECHNICAL NOTE ON RADIOGRAPHY OF FRAGMENTS

Char. Karakalos

The first radiographs of the Antikythera Mechanism were taken by means of a weak source of Thulium-170, after a request from the National Archaeological Museum of Athens to the Greek Atomic Energy Commission for the possibility of radiographical inspection of this valuable and unique relic of Greek antiquity.

The radiography laboratory of the National Research Center "Democritos," being then under development, was only equipped with elementary radio-isotope apparatus to meet nondestructive testing needs in industry.

In spite of the fact that the images taken by these means were of a fair quality, they showed some new gears in fragment A.

It appears then that systematic radiographic work on the pieces of the mechanism, with x-rays mainly, would be helpful for the understanding of its structure and function.

After the first testing with the Thulium-170 radiation source, the whole work was carried out with two portable x-ray units with similar characteristics, as follows:

(*a*) ANDREX, model 1631
    KV range, continuous regulation   50–160 KV
    mA range, continuous regulation   1–5 mA
    Effective focal spot size   1.5 × 1.5 mm
    Beam angle   40°

(*b*) FEDREX, model F 216F
    KV range, stepless   35–160 KV
    mA range, stepless   2–5 mA
    Focal spot size   1.5 × 1.5 mm
    Beam angle   40° × 56°

In order to fix the central ray perpendicular to the film, a standard specimen was used. An additional standard specimen proved useful for the comparison of some stereo-radiographic results. Appropriate devices have been constructed for an easy change of the focus-to-film-distance (F.F.D.) and the translation of the object for out of center shooting.

In order to control the image contrast of the radiographs two step-wedge indicators, made of copper sheets 2 mm thick, were used. The first was placed next to the object, and the second one, which consisted of three concentric small disks, was sometimes placed on the mechanism.

THE OBJECT. MATERIAL AND THICKNESS

The initial metal bronze out of which the mechanism was made is entirely transformed to decomposition products, squeezed together under great pressure, corroded, and covered with some calcareous accretions. The structure of the object itself is therefore inhomogeneous and very discontinuous, and the existence of many gaps makes the range of the radiographic thickness extremely large.

At an area of irregular size, about 16 × 18 cm, and in a space of thickness, nearly 24 mm, which is the gap within the drive wheel B1 and the back dial plate, are situated in various positions and levels, the 25 gear wheels, its supporting plates and other components of the main mechanism. There is not therefore any definite material thickness to be measured.

EXPOSURE CONDITIONS

A trial-and-error method has been used to determine the exposure conditions.

Film: Films of the Agfa-Gevaert Structurix type D7, D4, and D2 have been exclusively used with lead screens (0, 05 + 0.15 mm) for a film size of 20 × 25 cm and lead foils (0.02 mm) for films of smaller sizes. Films of smaller sizes were preferred for two reasons: (*a*) they are more suitable for a closer contact to the object, resulting in a sharper film image, (*b*) for partial exposure requirements.

Geometry: Focus-to-Film Distance: To make a whole radiograph of the largest fragment A, using a beam angle of 40°, a minimum F.F.D. of 23 cm is required. Lower distances than 23 cm give a partial view of the object. To attain the optimum result other working distances were also used, in a range varied from 17 to 150 cm.

Aspect selection: In most exposures the surface $A1$ (of the drive main wheel) faced the radiation beam. Fewer radiographs were taken with the object upside down, in order to minimize the distance of the upper gear wheels to the film.

Scatter Radiation: To reduce scatter radiation appropriate lead diaphragms were applied at the tube window which confined the radiation beam to the desired object area. Furthermore lead backing and, in some instances, lead masking techniques were used.

Kilovoltage selection and exposures: In view of the fact that the specimen is of a high object contrast, all the available alternative techniques have been used, viz.:

a) Individual partial views, of the significant areas of the object at the lowest tube high tension, in accordance to the thickness to be penetrated.
b) One exposure on two films with different speeds.
c) Low contrast producing technique for the entire mechanism exposure on a single film.

The Kilovoltage working value was therefore different each time, ranging from 110 to 160 Kv. As an exception in technique (*c*) a fixed tube potential of 160 Kv was used in preference. Table 6 that follows lists some typical exposures used for the four fragments of the mechanism assembly:

TABLE 6

Object	F. F. D. cm	H. T Kv	Expos. mA. min.	Type of film	Type of screens
Fragment A	140 cm	160 Kv	7	D 7	50/150 μ
Fragment B	30	150	1.15	D 4	50/150 μ
Fragment C	20	125	3.5	D 2	20/20 μ
Fragment D	50	120	20	D 2	20/20 μ

In order to find the level of the wheels the classical method of two exposures on a single film, by moving the x-ray tube, has been applied for the wheels $E1$, $B3$, $E2$ but without satisfactory results.

The overlapping image was so complicated that it was too difficult for the displacement to be measured. But the geometrical distortion of the radii of the gear wheels on the films taken at the smallest F.F.D. (17–23 cm) verify in general the already established positions.

RESULTS

From a fairly big number or radiographs taken, only the most suitable were chosen for detailed examination and the distances between the axes of the gear wheels, the diameters and the number of teeth were determined.

Determination of wheel diameters: Radiographs of a F.F.D. more than one meter were used to avoid geometrical distortion in order to determine the diameter of the wheels and the size of the other components of the mechanism.

Counting the number of gear teeth: The counting of the number of the gear teeth was made directly on the negative plates with the naked eye or with the help of a magnifying glass. In cases of doubt and for greater accuracy positive enlarged copies have been used.

On these copies the circumference of the gears has been drawn, the positions of the missing teeth have been measured in, and then all of the teeth-tips have been perforated with a pin.

The counting of the number of the gear teeth has been done by enumerating on the reverse side of the photograph the number of the corresponding holes. It is hoped that this method achieved the least errors.

All the radiographic exposure work has been carried out in the laboratories of the National Archaeological Museum of Athens with the x-ray apparatus of the National Research Council "Democritos."

In order to complete the radiometric examination I further intend to use a 250 Kv. x-ray unit for some more stereographic exposures and lateral shots.

I should like to thank the authorities of National Archaeological Museum of Athens and the Greek Atomic Energy Commission for permission and facilities granted to me.

INDEX

Aaboe, Asger, 3
Abi Bakr, Muhammed b., 42, 55
Allen, Elias, 52
Almagest, 19
Analysis, spectrochemical, 64
Anaphoric clock, 22, 40, 59
Annual cycle, 41
Antikythera (Island), 5
Antikythera youth, 8
Aphrodisias, 51
Arachne, 59
Aratus, 56
Archimedes, 13, 51, 53, 56, 57, 59, 60, 61, 62; clock of, 58; sphere of, 11
Aristotle, 53
Arnold, Asa, 61
Astrolabic water clocks, 54
Astronomy, Babylonian, 60
Atlas, 22
Atomic Energy Commission, Greek, 13
Automation, 60
Automaton theater, 60

Babylonian astronomy, 60
Bachelder, Myrtle, 66
Baldewin, Eberhart, 60, 61
Barulkos, 53, 54
Bastulus, 42
Bedini, Silvio, 55
von Bertele, H., 60
al-Biruni, 42, 54, 55, 59
Bobbin and fly frame, 61
Bol, Peter Cornelius, 9
Brass, 12
Brieux, Alain, 42
Bronze, 12
Bürgi, Jobst, 60, 61

Calendar reform, Julian, 11
Calendars, Egyptian rotating, 11; Alexandrian fixed, 11
Caley, Earle R., 63
Callipic cycle, 50, 57
Calypso (ship), 9
Casing of mechanism, 13, 14, 17
Cassiterite, 47
Chariots, south pointing, 60
Chelai, 17
Chemical analysis of metal fragments, 11, 63
Cicero, 9, 13, 56, 58, 59, 61, 62
Circles, divided, 20
Claudian, 57
Clepsydra, 22, 40
Clock, anaphoric, 22, 40, 59; of Archimedes, 58; cuckoo, 60; water, 59
Clocks (see Water clocks); mechanical, 54
Clockwork, 53
Computer, digital, 60; solar and lunar calendar, 54
Conservation of fragments, 10
Contrate wheel, 21, 27, 29, 40
Crank handle, 20, 40
Cuckoo clock, 60
Cycle, annual, 41; eclipse, 33, 44, 46; Metonic, 41, 43, 44, 50, 58

Dachs, Karl, 11
Damberge, 11, 63
Dating of fragments, 20
Dauthiau, 61
Delos, 9, 51
Demopoulos, General, 13
Dial, front, 16, 18; accuracy of division of zodiac scale, 19, 20; lower back, 15, 35; moon phase, 43; upper back, 15
Dial plates, 17, 20
Dial pointer, 15
Dial work, 13
Dials, back, 14; subsidiary, 15, 25
Diels, Hermann, 11
Differential gear system, 35, 45, 60
Differential turntable, 21, 40, 41, 44
Digital computer, 60
Dioptra, 53
Divided circles, 20
Division, uneven, 23, 24
de Dondi, Giovanni, 54, 55, 59, 60, 61
Door plate inscriptions, 49, 50
Doors, double, 21
Drachman, A. G., 20, 53, 59
Dudley, Darle W., 53
Dumas, Frederick, 9

Eclipse cycle, 33, 44, 46
Edwards, G. Roger, 8
Eichner, L. C., 35
Epagomenal days, 18
Ephesos, 9
Epicyclic gearing, 44
Epicycloid, 25, 54
Epigraphical evidence, 48
Equation of time, 61
Equilateral triangle, shape of gear teeth, 25, 54, 43
Equinox, autumnal, 18
Error, of graduation of divisions, 18; in radius, 25
Escapement, 54
Euctemon, 58
Eudoxos, 46, 49, 56

Farringdon, Benjamin, 51
Fiducial mark, 19, 20
Fink, C. G., and E. P. Poluskin, 66
Folding handle, 20
Fraction $\frac{1}{2}$, 50
Fragatos, Dr. G., 13
Fragment D, 13
Frost, Honor, 9

Gallus, Gaius Sulpicius, 56
Gamma radiography, 12, 13
Gear A, 27
Gear $B1$, 27
Gear $B2$, 28
Gears $B3$ and $B4$, 28
Gears $C1$ and $C2$, 29
Gear $D2$, 32
Gears $E1$, and $E2$, 32
Gears $E3$ and $E4$, 32
Gear $E5$, 34
Gears $F1$ & $F2$, 35

Gears $G1$ and $G2$, 35
Gears $H1$ and $H2$, 35
Gear I, 35
Gear J, 35
Gears $K1$ and $K2$, 35
Gears $L1$ and $L2$, 36
Gears $M1$ and $M2$, 36
Gear N, 36
Gears $O1$ and $O2$, 36
Gearing, epicyclic, 44; planetary, 21
Gearing system, sectional diagram of, 43
Gear system, differential, 35, 45, 60
Gear teeth as function of wheel radius, 41
Gear teeth numbers, accuracy of estimating, 22
Gear wheel, toothed, 53
Geminos, 46, 49, 62
Gibbs, Sharon L., 51
Glyphadia, Point, 5
Grace, Virginia R., 8
Greco-Egyptian year, 18
Greek jewelry, 54
Green (tinsmith), 61
Gunther, Robert T., 11

Handle, crank, 20, 40; folding, 20
Hartner, Willy, 11
Hauser, Fritz, 58
Heliacal risings and settings, 18
Hellenistic pottery, date of, 8
Herculaneum, 51
Hermes, 9
Heron, 35, 53, 54, 58, 60
High Technology, 52, 53, 54
Hipparchus, 19, 59
Hodometer, 35, 53
Hoffman, H., and T. F. Davidson, 54
de Honnicourt, Villard, 52
Hooke, Robert, 52
Houldsworth, Henry, 61
Hyades, 49

Industrial Revolution, 52, 53
Input axle, 21
Inscriptions, 12, 46; door plate, 49, 50; mirror image, 14, 16, 21, 47
Invention of complicated clockwork, 60
Isagoge, 49, 62
Isis festival, 49

al-Jazari, 58
Joins of fragments, 13, 14, 47
Jovanovic, Stanka, 66

Kallipic (see Callipic)
Kallipolitis, Director, 13
Kappos, Dr. D. A., 13
Karakalos, Dr. Ch., 3, 13, 66
Karakalos, Emily, 13
Karo, George, 12
Karouzos, Christos, 12, 63
Keskinto, 62
Key letters, 20
Kondos, Demetrios El., 5, 8
Kos, 9

69

Ktesibios, 53, 54, 56, 58
Kyrrhestes, Andronicus, 40, 51, 62

Lactantius, 57
Leibniz, 60
Leonardo da Vinci, 52, 55, 60, 61
Leskowitz, Ann, 3
Letters, of the alphabet, 18; on the limb, 49
Libra, 17, 18, 20
Lindos, 62
Lloyd, H. Alan, 60
Low Technology, 52

Maddison, Francis, 55
Mahdia, 9
Maltezos, K., 11
Manitius, 49
Marbles, date of, 9
Marcellus, Marcus, 56
Mathematical practitioners, 52
Matschoss, Conrad, 53
Maudsley, 61
Mechanical clocks, 54
Mechanism assemblies, 20
Meritt, Benjamin, 48
Metallurgical microphotographs, 65
Metonic cycle, 41, 43, 44, 50, 58
Miller, F. J., E. V. Sayre, and B. Keisch, 12
Millwright, 54
Mirror image inscriptions, 14, 16, 21, 47
Mithraditic wars, 9
Molon, 56
Month, synodic, 42
Moon indicator, 40
Moon phase volvelle, 43
Museum, Greek Archaeological, 8; Greek National, 13
Mykale, 8

Nastulus, 42
Needham, Joseph, 53, 60
Neugebauer, Otto, 3, 59
Nielson, Betty, 66
Noble, Joseph, 52

Octoëteris, 41
Oikonomu, A., 8
Orientation of the zodiac, 21
Ovid, 57

Pachon, 11, 18, 19, 20
Parapegma, 16, 17, 18, 20, 21, 22, 46, 49
Paros, 9
Pascal, 60
Payni, 18, 19

Peg and wedge construction, 35
Philon, 58
Philoponus, 10
Pinakakia, 6
Pinion $D1$, 29, 30
Planetary gearing, 21
Plate, back dial, 21; back door, 21; back door, inscription, 47; back main, 21; front door, 20, 22; front main, 21
Plates, arrangement of, 20; indicator, sun and moon, 21
Plato, 11
Plutarch, 51
Pompeii, 51
Pope, Beverly, 3
Posidonios, 9, 13, 56, 57, 59, 61, 62
Potamo, Port, 5
Practitioners, mathematical, 52
Price, D. de Solla, 52, 53
Projection, stereographic, 59
Ptolemy, 11, 19
Publication, definitive, of Antikythera treasure, 11
Published account, first, 10

Qualitative chemical analysis, 63

Radiographs, 29
Radiography, gamma, 12, 13
Rados, Konstantin, 10, 11
Ralph, Elizabeth K., 8
Reconstruction, preliminary, 12
Rediadis, Perikles, 8, 10, 11, 14, 63
Rehm, Albert, 11, 14, 49
Revolution, Scientific, 52, 53
Rhodes, 9, 13, 49, 51, 56, 62
Richard of Wallingford, 55, 59, 61
Ridwan, 58
Roberts, Richard, 61
Robinson, Henry S., 8
Robots, 60
Rousopoulos, 10
Royal Society of London, 52
Rupp, Dr. A. F., 13

Salzburg plate, 59
a San Cajetano, Aureliano and David, 61
Schlachter, A., 11
Scientific Revolution, 52, 53
Sectional diagram of gearing system, 43
Ship's instruments, 22
Shipwreck, date of, 8
Siderial revolutions, 42
Sleeswyk, Prof. A. W., 32
Smith, Cyril Stanley, 54, 63, 64
Solar and lunar calendar computer, 54
Solder, 27, 35, 63

South-pointing chariots, 60
Spacers, 28
Spectrochemical analysis, 64
Staïs, Spyridon, 8, 9, 10, 11
Statues, date and provenance of, 8
Stadiatis, Elias, 5, 8
Stamires, Dr. George, 12
Stereographic projection, 59
Subsidiary dials, 15, 25
Sundials, 51
Svoronos, J. N., 8, 9, 10, 11, 47
Syme, 5
Synodic month, 42
Synodic motion, Moon, 41
Synodic phenomena, 41

Tenos, 62
Thales, 56
Theophanidis, Jean, 9, 11, 12, 20
Throckmorton, Peter, 8
Tidal dials, 61
Toomer, Gerald, 3
Tower of Winds, 22, 40, 51, 54, 59, 60
Turntable, differential, 21, 40, 41, 44

Uneven division, 23, 24
Urania, 22

da Vinci, Leonardo, 52, 55, 60, 61
Virgo, 17, 18
Vitruvius, 53, 54, 59
Vlikada, Point, 5

Wang, Ling, 53
Washer, 28
Water clock, 59
Water clocks, astrolabic, 54
Watt, James, 52
Wedge and peg construction, 35
Weight drive, 54
Weinberg, Dr. Alvin, 13
Weinberg, Gladys, 8, 12
Werner, Dr. A. E., 47
Wheel, contrate, 21, 27, 29, 40; main drive, 21, 40
Wiedemann, Eilhard, 42, 58
Wilhelm, 9, 10
Williamson, Joseph, 61
Wu Tê-Jen, 60

X-ray investigation, 12, 13

Yalouris, Dr. N., 13
Yen-Su, 60

Zinner, Ernst, 11, 12, 47
Zodiac, 17; orientation of, 21

Q
11
P6
n.s.
v.64
pt.7

MAY 14 1975